к

C000021777

Karl Marx is the most important modern philosopher. His work has radically changed the course of world history, continental philosophy, political theory, literary criticism, and cultural studies. The sheer range of his achievements, and the depth of his critical insights, continue to speak to our present moment. This book places Marx's writings in their historical context, providing a clear guide to his key ideas and intellectual legacy. Written for both students and scholars, it illustrates Marx's ideas with examples drawn from William Shakespeare, Herman Melville, Leo Tolstoy, Bertolt Brecht, Theodor Dreiser, Thomas Pynchon, Toni Morrison, Sally Rooney, Claude McKay, Tennessee Williams, *Mad Men*, and *Margin Call*.

Key ideas discussed in this guide include:

- Tracing historical contexts and developments in Marx's work over his lifetime
- Focusing on Marxism as an interpretative strategy, paying special attention to its impact on literary criticism and cultural studies
- Examining recent developments in Marxist theory, such as a stronger focus on the environment, climate crisis, and world ecology
- Exploring the continued relevance of Marx and Marxism today.

This Routledge Critical Thinkers guide will enable readers to critically assess and interpret Marx's major works, while also introducing his methods of critical analysis. Preparing readers to approach his original texts, this guide ensures that readers of all levels will find Marx accessible, challenging, and of continued relevance.

Andrew Rowcroft offers a comprehensive introduction to Marx's revolutionary ideas, examining the influence Marx had on literary studies, cultural studies, modernism, and philosophy.

Andrew Rowcroft is Lecturer in English at the University of Lincoln, UK. His forthcoming book is titled *Marxism and the Contemporary*.

ROUTLEDGE CRITICAL THINKERS

Series Editor: Robert Eaglestone, Royal Holloway, University of London, UK

Routledge Critical Thinkers is a series of accessible introductions to key figures in contemporary critical thought.

With a unique focus on historical and intellectual contexts, the volumes in this series examine important theorists':

- significance
- motivation
- key ideas and their sources
- impact on other thinkers

Concluding with extensively annotated guides to further reading, *Routledge Critical Thinkers* are the student's passport to today's most exciting critical thought.

Also available in the series:

For more information about this series, please visit: www.routledge.com/Routledge-Critical-Thinkers/book-series/SE0370

KARL MARX

Andrew Rowcroft

Routledge
Taylor & Francis Group

LONDON AND NEW YORK

First published 2021
by Routledge
2 Park Square, Milton Park, Abingdon, Oxon OX14 4RN

and by Routledge
605 Third Avenue, New York, NY 10158

Routledge is an imprint of the Taylor & Francis Group, an informa business

British Library Cataloguing-in-Publication Data
A catalogue record for this book is available from the British Library

Library of Congress Cataloging-in-Publication Data
Names: Rowcroft, Andrew, author.
Title: Karl Marx / Andrew Rowcroft.
Description: Abingdon, Oxon; New York, NY : Routledge, 2021. | Includes bibliographical references and index.
Identifiers: LCCN 2020048269 | ISBN 9780367406028 (hardback) | ISBN 9780367406189 (paperback) | ISBN 9780429357022 (ebook)
Subjects: LCSH: Marx, Karl, 1818–1883. | Philosophy, Marxist. | Communism. | Philosophers–Germany–Biography.
Classification: LCC B3305.M74 R66 2021 | DDC 335.4092–dc23
LC record available at https://lccn.loc.gov/2020048269

ISBN: 978-0-367-40602-8 (hbk)
ISBN: 978-0-367-40618-9 (pbk)
ISBN: 978-0-429-35702-2 (ebk)

Typeset in Sabon
by Newgen Publishing UK

CONTENTS

SERIES EDITOR'S PREFACE

The books in this series offer introductions to major critical thinkers who have influenced literary studies and the humanities. The *Routledge Critical Thinkers* series provides the books you can turn to first when a new name or concept appears in your studies.

Each book will equip you to approach a key thinker's original texts by explaining their key ideas, putting them into context and, perhaps most importantly, showing you why this thinker is considered to be significant. The emphasis is on concise, clearly written guides that do not presuppose specialist knowledge. Although the focus is on particular figures, the series stresses that no critical thinker ever existed in a vacuum, but instead emerged from a broader intellectual, cultural, and social history. Finally, these books will act as a bridge between you and the thinkers' original texts: not replacing them, but rather complementing what they wrote. In some cases, volumes consider small clusters of thinkers working in the same area, developing similar ideas, or influencing each other.

These books are necessary for a number of reasons. In his 1997 autobiography, *Not Entitled*, the literary critic Frank Kermode wrote of a time in the 1960s:

> On beautiful summer lawns, young people lay together all night, recovering from their daytime exertions and listening to a troupe of Balinese musicians. Under their blankets or their sleeping bags, they would chat drowsily about the gurus of the time ... What they repeated was largely hearsay; hence my lunchtime suggestion, quite impromptu, for a series of short, very cheap books offering authoritative but intelligible introductions to such figures.

There is still a need for 'authoritative and intelligible introductions'. But this series reflects a different world from the 1960s. New thinkers have emerged and the reputations of others have risen and fallen as new research has developed. New methodologies and challenging ideas have spread through the arts and humanities. The study of literature is no longer – if it ever was – simply the study and evaluation of poems, novels, and plays. It is also the study of ideas, issues, and difficulties that arise in any literary text and in its interpretation. Other arts and humanities subjects have changed in analogous ways.

With these changes, new problems have emerged. The ideas and issues behind these radical changes in the humanities are often presented without reference to wider contexts, or as theories which you can simply 'add on' to the texts you read. Certainly, there's nothing wrong with picking out selected ideas or using what comes to hand – indeed, some thinkers have argued that this is, in fact, all we can do. However, it is sometimes forgotten that each new idea comes from the pattern and development of somebody's thought, and it is important to study the range and context of their ideas. Against theories 'floating in space', the *Routledge Critical Thinkers* series places key thinkers and their ideas firmly back in their context.

More than this, these books reflect the need to go back to the thinkers' own texts and ideas. Every interpretation of an idea, even the seemingly most innocent one, offers you its own 'spin', implicitly or explicitly. To read only books about a thinker, rather than texts by that thinker, is to deny yourself the chance of making up your own mind. Sometimes what makes a significant figure's work difficult to approach is not so much its style or content, as the feeling of not knowing where to start. The purpose of these books is to give you a 'way in' by offering an accessible overview of these thinkers' ideas and works and by guiding your further reading, starting with each thinker's own texts. To use a metaphor from the philosopher Ludwig Wittgenstein (1889–1951), these books are ladders, to be thrown away after you have climbed to the next level. Not only do they equip you to approach new ideas, but they also empower you, by leading you back to the theorist's own texts and encouraging you to develop your own informed opinions.

Finally, these books are necessary because, just as intellectual needs have changed, education systems around the world – the contexts in which introductory books are usually read – have changed radically, too. What was suitable for the minority higher education systems of the 1960s is not suitable for the larger, wider, more diverse, high-technology education systems of the twenty-first century. These changes call not just for new, up-to-date introductions, but for new methods of presentation. The presentational aspects of *Routledge Critical Thinkers* have been developed with today's students in mind.

Each book in the series has a similar structure. It begins with a section offering an overview of the life and ideas of the featured thinker or thinkers and explaining why they are important. The central section of each book discusses the thinkers' key ideas, their context, evolution, and reception; for books that deal with more than one thinker, they also explain and explore the influence of each on each. Each volume concludes with a survey of the impact of the thinker or thinkers, outlining how their ideas have been taken up and developed by others. In addition, there is a detailed final section suggesting and describing books for further reading. This section forms an integral part of each volume, offering brief descriptions of the thinkers' key works followed by information on the most useful critical works and, in some cases, on relevant websites. This section will guide you in your reading, enabling you to follow your interests and develop your own projects. Throughout each book, references are given in what is known as the Harvard system (the author and date of a work cited are given in the text, and you can look up the full details in the References at the back). This offers a lot of information in very little space. The books also explain technical terms and use boxes to describe events or ideas in more detail, away from the main emphasis of the discussion. Boxes are also used to highlight definitions of terms frequently used or coined by a thinker. In this way, the boxes serve as a kind of glossary, easily identified when flicking through the book.

The thinkers in the series are 'critical' for three reasons. First, they are examined in the light of subjects that involve criticism: principally literary studies or English and cultural studies, but also other disciplines that rely on the criticism of books, ideas, theories, and unquestioned assumptions. Secondly, they are critical because studying their work will provide you with a 'toolkit' for your own informed critical reading and thought, which will make you critical. Third, these thinkers are critical because they are crucially important: they deal with ideas and questions that can overturn conventional understandings of the world, of texts, of everything we take for granted, leaving us with a deeper understanding of what we already knew, and with new ideas.

No introduction can tell you everything. However, by offering a way into critical thinking, this series hopes to begin to engage you in an activity which is productive, constructive, and potentially life-changing.

ACKNOWLEDGEMENTS

My thanks to Bob Eaglestone, Lucie Armitt, Scott Brewster, Owen Clayton, Christopher Marlow, Jason Whittaker, and John F. Davies.

WHY MARX?

Karl Marx (1818–1883) is the most important intellectual figure of recent times. He is also the most controversial, although nearly always for the wrong reasons. A German philosopher, journalist, critic, and revolutionary, he arrived at stunning, innovative conclusions about class, capital, communism, revolution, ideology, economy, ecology, nature, idealism, materialism, humanism, and the state. His ideas were the impetus for political movements that shaped the twentieth century and laid the basis for the creation of societies which claimed a commitment to his principles. Marx is unique because he uncovered structural connections between seemingly distinct areas, which is why his work ranges from philosophy to literary criticism, from economics to history. He is not only the most famous communist and revolutionary, but he also embodied the idea of revolution in his work, creating radical approaches to seeing the world.

Marx's ability to make powerful connections between different aspects of life led to his investigation of capitalism. For Marx, capitalism is above all else a system of exploitation, prone to instability, and crisis. Political economists, Marx noted, liked to begin with the supposedly "natural" state of humanity, which they imagined to be like that of Robinson Crusoe shipwrecked on an island, in the novel by Daniel Defoe (1660–1731). But alone on his island, Crusoe does not represent the real conditions of society. In his major three-volume work, *Capital* (1867–1894), Marx embarks on a critique of political economy which exposes the limitations of arguments which deal in phenomena in isolation. He argued these other approaches were unimaginative because they could not see that each 'individual's production is dependent on the production of all others' (Marx, 1993, 83). For Marx, by thinking in terms of fundamental processes, rather than isolated fragments, we see not 'the chaotic conception of a whole, but a rich totality of many determinations and relations' (Marx, 1993, 100). Drawing upon concepts developed by another German philosopher, G.W.F Hegel (1770–1831), Marx aimed to create a complete picture of capitalism, to accurately represent a complex economic system ever in full movement, dynamic expansion, and perpetual breakdown. Marx chronicled both the horrors and achievements of capitalism and conceived of a radical, emancipatory future, which he called communism.

We can see the horrors and achievements of the capitalist in *Sister Carrie* (1900) by Theodore Dreiser (1871–1945). This novel depicts the hardships of factory work, showing it to be empty, tedious, and bleak. In Dreiser's narrative, Carrie, after spending an exhausting day searching for work, finally gets a job at a shoe factory. 'Her neck and shoulders ached in bending over' her machine, we are told: 'Her hands began to ache at the wrists and then at the fingers, and toward the last she seemed one mass of dull complaining muscles, fixed in an eternal position and performing a single mechanical movement which became more and more distasteful until at last it was absolutely nauseating' (Dreiser, 1981, 38–39). As Carrie sits at the machine making shoes:

> she felt she could hardly endure such a life. Her idea of work had been so entirely different. All during the long afternoon she thought of the city outside with its imposing show, crowds and fine buildings [...] By three o'clock she was sure it must be six, and by four it seemed as if they had forgotten to note the hour and were letting all work overtime
>
> (Dreiser, 1981, 40–41).

At the end of her working day, Carrie 'felt a slight relief, but it was only at her escape' from her drudgery (Dreiser 1981, 41).

Marx provides a critical framework for understanding how Carrie is exploited. Forced into backbreaking work she undergoes a process called alienation. Alienation describes the ways in which Carrie is torn from her human essence or potential by work. First, she is alienated from herself, turned into an automaton doing a 'single mechanical movement' over and over again; second, she is alienated from the products of her labour, the shoes she makes, which bear nothing of her on them; third, she is alienated from her engagement in free conscious activity, and can only image the delights of the 'show, crowds, and fine buildings' outside; finally she is alienated from the other workers, as the factory foreman ensures a strict silence while working. Her pain and fatigue are a direct result of the ways in which, under capitalism, jobs are broken down into mind-numbing tasks to maximise profit at all points along the commodity chain.

Marx diagnosed alienation from four points of view, all of which are present in the example given above. But they are all part of a single reality. Marx argued that, in a capitalist society, we are forced to surrender our time, energy, even our humanity, to wage-labour. One of the most important aspects of alienation is the way in which workers are removed from the product of their labour, which they are not allowed to keep. This means, for Marx, that the 'object which labour produces – labour's product – confronts it as something *alien*, as a power *independent* of the producer' (Marx, *MECW3*, 272). Whether it is pouring pints in a pub, stacking shelves in a supermarket, or making shoes in a factory, workers do not work for themselves, but 'must sacrifice their time and carry out slave-labour, completely losing their freedom, in the service of greed' (Marx, *MECW3*, 237). Marx saw that this kind of work, often taking place in the factories or fields, and even done by children, is 'exhausting, physically destructive and morally and intellectually crippling labour' (Marx and Engels, 1992, 292). Capitalism, Marx discovered, is a system that impoverishes the worker and benefits the capitalist. In contrast, Marx wanted to move beyond capitalism to a realm of individual freedom. He was not against work; indeed, he understood it to be a vital activity in human life and, when done well, a fulfilling and liberating activity. He famously talked of a utopian society in which 'nobody has one exclusive sphere of activity but each can become accomplished in any branch he wishes': such an individual 'could do one thing today and another tomorrow, to hunt in the morning, fish in the afternoon, rear cattle in the evening [and] criticise after dinner' (Marx, *MECW5*, 47). Marx objected to work under capitalism because it degrades the worker (and the capitalist).

As this reading of *Sister Carrie* shows, we can use Marx's observations about capitalism to unpack the complexities of literary texts. As this book will show, literature offer a series of unique opportunities for reflecting on the social, political, cultural, and environmental challenges of today. Marx was aware of this, peppering his works with references to literary works, and even using literature to think through his key ideas. In this book, I will be using examples from art, literature, and culture to illustrate Marx's ideas, reveal his achievements, and show the depth of his critical insights.

Before going further, I must make an important distinction between Marx and Marxism. Much – but certainly not all! – of what we mean when we say Marxism are a set of approaches to Marx's works developed by his lifelong friend Friedrich Engels (1820–1895) and later revolutionaries, such as Vladimir Lenin (1870–1924). After Marx's death in 1883, Engels wanted to present all of Marx's unpublished work to the world. This was a very difficult task, for two reasons. Firstly, Marx's handwriting was terrible (Marx tried to get a job as a railway clerk in 1862 but was rejected for bad handwriting). Secondly, his manuscripts were unorganised (a Prussian spy once broke into the house and noted the condition of Marx's office, with books and papers strewn everywhere). Engel had to put together unfinished materials, publish unpublished texts, and translate work into English. We have Engels to thank for bringing Marx's work to the world, but his editorial efforts have produced problems. Engels also published his own works, which I will discuss in the 'After Marx' section, which, in their effort to showcase Marx's ideas, often reduced them to core tenants. This book, however, deals almost exclusively with Marx, not the history of Marxism.

Marx's most important work is *Capital*. It took eighteen years to write, went largely ignored when it was published, and Marx only finished the first volume before his death (Engels edited the final two). *Capital* set out the laws of the motion of capitalism, revealing how and why it works. Many are put off from reading *Capital* because they believe it to be a book about economics. Marx deals with economic matters, but he is much more than an economist (no offence to economists). As David Harvey (1935-) argues, *Capital* is an 'astonishingly rich book' with Marx using the works of Shakespeare, Faust, fairy tales, werewolves, vampires, and poetry to tell his story (Harvey, 2010, 2). It reflects a period of incredibly intense research, where Marx studied in the Reading Room of the British Museum, while living in London. *Capital* is like a modernist novel, with hundreds of characters, open-ended symbols, and the juxtaposition of different voices and quotations. The first volume is a work of world literature, with references to the Bible, Goethe, Milton, Homer, Horace, Balzac, Dante, Schiller, Sophocles, Plato, Defoe, Cervantes, Dryden, Heine, Virgil, Thomas More, and Samuel Butler, alongside allusions to romantic novels, pulp literature, popular ballads, songs, jingles, melodrama, myth, and proverbs.

If *Capital* marries a rich range of literary allusions, it has also been read in remarkably different ways, supporting a range of varied approaches and interpretations. One scholar has recently argued that Marx's book mirrors the *Divine Comedy* (1321), by the Italian poet Dante (d.1321), which involves a journey through hell, the rejection of sin, and the search for redemption (Roberts, 2017, 257). What I will show throughout this book is that Marx is not only a great philosopher and critic but a literary craftsman. For anyone interested in history, politics, economics, philosophy, or literature, *Capital* is a vital and fascinating text. It is a pleasure to read, but also complex and challenging. I will introduce and explain this work, but also, at the back of this book, I will provide a list of further reading to assist you.

THIS BOOK

This book features ten short chapters. It is meant to be read in full, but each individual chapter is a self-contained unit, so you can dip into individual chapters if you wish or use them as a refresher later. Marx's career as a communist and revolutionary meant a life of poverty, hardship, and toil. He never held an academic post at a University, was chased out of most of the countries in Europe and lost most of his children to diseases contracted by dreadful living conditions. Despite this, he led a fascinating life, was a passionate intellectual and critic, and wrote works which challenged received ideas. Chapter One gives a brief history of Marx's life. Chapter Two reveals the sources of Marx's ideas. Marx read voraciously, across many disciplines, but his major influence was the work of Hegel. It may seem strange to mention Hegel in a book on Marx. But Hegel inspired Marx to develop his own ideas on history, human nature, materialism, the state, and to use a mode of argument called dialectics. An account of this influence is therefore essential.

Chapter Three introduces the *Communist Manifesto* (1848). Marx is the world's most famous communist and communism forms the central political idea of his thought. Marx's spent a lifetime developing his thoughts, but his key ideas (on capital, class, communism, and revolution) can all be located in this one text. The *Manifesto* presents the principles of the newly formed Communist Party, but it is much more than a political document. In it, Marx shows that communism is a radical idea with a rich philosophical meaning. This chapter explores the major ideas of the *Manifesto* and connects them to important concepts that will inform the rest of the book.

Chapter Four introduces *Capital*. For students of English, *Capital* is a text full of secrets, symbols, enigmas, riddles, narrative styles, and allusions. To consider *Capital* a literary text that requires close reading in no way detracts from the political arguments that Marx makes. I will discuss capital, the commodity, labour, value, and the working day but I also want to pay close attention to *Capital* as a narrative, as a rich multi-layered masterpiece. Chapter Five builds on this, turning to Marx's concern with literature, capitalism, and ideology. Marx's work has literary qualities, and he relied on literature to represent the different dimensions of capitalism. Literature, for Marx, was a force for the transformation of the world.

Chapter Six explores one of Marx's most important ideas: the relationship between economics and culture, or the base and superstructure. This idea is particularly important in literary and cultural studies, which is concerned with thinking about the ways in which texts simultaneously reflect, represent, and express the world. Chapter Seven examines Marx's views on history and historical development. He never used the term 'historical materialism' (it was used by Engels) but he did labour to understand the vast historical shifts taking place in his lifetime. In a range of texts, Marx showed how history proceeds through a series of different modes of production, characterised by complex class struggles that culminate in the break-down of capitalism and the emergence of communism. Chapter Eight will introduce Marx's ideas on class. Marx understood capitalism as a mode of production in which one class systematically extracts profit from another. To overcome capitalism, struggle between classes was essential. Chapter Nine turns to new and exciting directions in Marx scholarship, focusing on Marx and nature. It is often assumed that Marx was a philosopher who had little to say about the environment. But it has become clear in recent years that Marx's work has a strong ecological dimension, and that he was interested in both ecology and economy. Chapter Ten presents Marx vision of a post-capitalist world, introducing ideas which are not contained in the *Manifesto*, which was written when he was a young man. 'After Marx' surveys the most important intellectual developments occurring after Marx's death. Focused primarily on literary criticism and cultural studies, it will introduce the work of key theorists and movements, alongside some important historical contexts that have helped shape this critique. The book ends with a 'Further Reading' section, which begins by listing Marx's works and providing some comments on each. Secondary texts are then given, but the emphasis is on how they illuminate the primary material, rather than Marxism itself.

It is my hope that this book will send the reader back to Marx, there to construct a more meaningful understanding of their own moment: a moment that, still, seems to be that of Karl Marx.

KEY IDEAS

1

BIOGRAPHY

Marx was born in Trier, a small cathedral city in the south west of Germany, on 5 May 1818. He was the child of Jewish parents who later converted to Christianity. His father was a successful lawyer, and Marx was raised in a comfortable liberal household. But, in Marx's time, liberals were a fairly radical bunch, given that the vast majority of established 'rulers were monarchs, or ruled as monarchs, and thus as authorities and authoritarians' (Carver, 2003, 121). Often expressing sentiments that were deeply anti-monarchical, anti-state, and anti-Christian, liberals were the rebels of their day and were considered a threat to the Prussian state.

The Marx family were affected by the French Revolution (1789–1799) and the Napoleonic Wars (1803–1815). Marx's father, Heinrich, was only able to qualify as a lawyer because of the educational initiatives of Napoleon; at the same time, he had to change his religion due to an increasingly restrictive policy towards Prussian Jews. The French Revolution had promised government, freedom, liberty, and equality. It had overthrown a discredited monarchy with a new republic. Three years before Marx's birth, Napoleon had been defeated at the Battle of Waterloo, a major offensive won by British and Prussian troops. These events shaped the structure of the world that Marx would inherit. Revolution was a real force for change.

From the age of twelve onward, Marx attended the local high school where he received a humanist education and wrote essays about the importance of working in the service of humanity. After school, Marx spent a year studying law at the University of Bonn. He attended lectures on philosophy, law, and literature, but politics was absent. After the revolution in France and the Napoleonic wars, German universities were keen to avoid unrest. Bonn was considered a potential hotspot of radicalism, but Marx had little interest in politics in this period.

Marx's student life was characterised by debt, drunkenness, and the writing of romantic poetry. He was a boisterous in his behaviour. He was wounded above the left eye in a duel and imprisoned by the university for being drunk and disturbing the peace. In letters to his father, Marx often pleads for more money to supplement his lifestyle. Heinrich was annoyed by these requests, and was increasingly concerned with Marx's bad habits, writing with evident distaste about his son's lack of realism, 'disorderliness, musty excursions into all departments of knowledge, musty brooding under a gloomy oil-lamp; running wild in a scholar's dressing gown and with unkempt hair' (Marx, *MECW1*, 688). His father complained about Marx's inability to keep the family informed of his activities, his drinking too much, and his spending money.

At his father's request, Marx moved his studies from Bonn to Berlin, a much larger university. Berlin was quickly becoming a new centre of cultural and intellectual activity, with radical publications and discussions circulating in coffee houses and beer halls. Marx revelled in this new environment, stimulated by the intellectual atmosphere of free and open debate. On 10 November 1837, Marx began a letter to his father. It is full of lofty philosophical prose. In it, Marx attempts to assure his father that he is a dutiful son. His early interest in poetry, he notes, 'was purely idealistic' (Marx, *MECW1*, 11). In the letter, Marx mentions that he has turned from writing (bad) poetry to studying law, and has made extensive notes from legal literature. But this study of law impelled him to turn to philosophy, a subject he considered much more interesting. Fascinated by philosophy, Marx had 'spent many a sleepless night, fought many a battle, and endured much

[...] excitement' (Marx, *MECW1*, 18). Fearing for his health, a doctor prescribed a visit to the country, which Marx turned into an opportunity to read the work of Hegel. Marx had already read Hegel, but at first the 'grotesque craggy melody' did not appeal to him (Marx, *MECW1*, 18). Reading Hegel a second time proved to be a major moment in Marx's life. I will explore the connection between the two in Chapter Two.

Marx's letter puzzled his father. In moving Marx to Berlin, Heinrich had hoped his son would receive an education that would lead to a profession and a secure income. Marx's admission that he had turned from law to philosophy could not have come at a worse time. Marx's father had become progressively, gravely ill. In May 1838 Heinrich died, and this loss affected Marx deeply.

THE DOCTOR'S CLUB

In Berlin, Marx joined the 'Doctor's Club', a group of young men who enjoyed drinking and philosophy. Most members held doctorates, hence the title. Members of the group included the philosophers Bruno Bauer (1809–1882) and Arnold Ruge (1802–1880).

Hegel was the central point of interest for the group. Hegel had held the chair of Philosophy at Berlin until his death in 1831 and was still the major figure in German philosophy. Marx's reading of Hegel was not unaided: he was assisted by other members of the Doctor's Club, one of whom, Eduard Gans (1797–1839), had known Hegel well. Marx's intellectual engagement with Hegel was intense and encompassing. The two never met, but Marx's indebtedness to Hegel was a kind of collaboration. Marx regularly turned to Hegel for a fundamental armature in ideas and methods, even while disagreeing with him and later claiming he had overturned or inverted Hegel's idealism. Hegel lives on every page that Marx wrote.

IDEALISM

Idealism is a diverse group of views which assert that reality is constituted through human perception, and therefore closely connected to ideas about the world. For idealists, mental categories (the mind, spirit, reason, or will) are the foundation of all reality and, although something independent of the mind is conceded, what we know about the world must all come through the constructive activities of our own mind. In Germany, major idealist thinkers include Immanuel Kant (1724–1804), Johann Gottlieb Fichte (1762–1814), Friedrich Wilhelm Joseph Schelling (1775–1854), and Hegel.

DR MARX

Marx wanted to be an academic, and for that he would need a doctorate. He completed his dissertation on the Greek philosopher Epicurus (341–270 BCE). Due to his need to secure a position, Marx wrote quickly and made some unnecessary attacks on the work of established thinkers: a dangerous move given the problems of attaining an academic post in Germany. His doctorate was conferred by the University of Jena in April 1841.

Afterwards, Marx moved back to Bonn, the city where his friend Bruno Bauer was now teaching. Marx had harboured hopes of a teaching appointment at the same university. But in March 1842, Bauer was dismissed for atheism. Without the help of Bauer, Marx had no hope of working at a university. There was, however, one other opportunity for Marx during this period.

MARX AND THE *RHEINISCHE ZEITUNG*

In the same year, Marx began working for a newspaper in Cologne, the *Rheinische Zeitung*. Within six months he became editor. Marx wrote articles on press freedom and wood theft. These texts were not journalism in the sense that we now understand the term. Marx undertook no investigative reporting, but blended his philosophical interests with real events. The *Rheinische Zeitung* advertised itself as a liberal newspaper, but it took a sharper turn under Marx's editorship. Letters from government officials were sent to the Prussian Censorship Minister claiming the paper was full of 'impudent and disrespectful criticism of the existing government institutions' (Marx, *MECW1*, 747). But Marx's articles are rich, passionate, and brimming with a desire for political justice. For the first time, Marx was concerned with practical political issues, turning philosophical insight towards solving socioeconomic problems.

ARTICLES ON WOOD THEFT

The best known of Marx's articles for the paper were those on the theft of wood. In his article 'Debates on the Law and the Theft of Wood' (1842), Marx made clear his disgust at the criminalisation of wood gathering. Traditionally, peasants and workers had been able to gather dead wood on the forest floor, which they had used for fires and thatching roofs. Wood shortages had led to tighter controls. Anyone now found to be gathering dead wood would be treated harshly, with offenders being compelled to carry out forced labour for forest owners. As Marx observed, Christian charity made way for a vicious materialism which would force an entire class of people into unpaid forestry work. Driven by hunger and hardship to collect wood, the poor once had a right to subsistence. Now, it was theft. This issue prompted Marx to think about economics. He began to understand that property, production, and issues of class were central to social relationships, and that the claims of religion, charity, and the state were mystifications that covered this up. He realised it was the daily concerns of humans – their social and material existence – that give meaning, shape, and coherence to their life. That is, he began to think as a *materialist*.

MATERIALISM

Materialism is a form of philosophy that focuses on matter as the fundamental substance in nature, and argues that seemingly non-material aspects – such as mental states and consciousness – are the result of the interaction of material relations. This approach is distinct to idealism, which holds that ideas are the dominant driving force of change, and that the world is, in some sense, mentally constructed. In response to Hegel's idealism, Marx had a materialist conception of the world, meaning he thought human existence is primarily a physical matter. Marx's materialist conception of reality was also a way of acknowledging the importance of transformative economic activity. Humans are material beings who live in a social world that is material in its actuality. For Marx, materialism is the vantage point of the collectively lived experience of social relations rather than individual consciousness.

As editor of the *Rheinische Zeitung,* Marx had marshalled his efforts towards drawing attention to the injustices of his time. Frequent attacks on the authorities led to the paper being shut down in April 1843. Marx embraced this with some optimism, contending that the lengthy battles with Prussian censors had taken up too much of his time. He was eager to leave Germany and start work on something new. Along with his articles, Marx's major writing during this time was the *Critique of Hegel's Philosophy of Right* (1843). In this text, Marx constructs a critical commentary on Hegel's political theory through a detailed, almost line-by-line textual analysis. Marx criticises Hegel and existing political institutions, attacking constitutional monarchy, landed estates, and primogeniture (the right of inheritance to the firstborn son). In both the *Critique* and his articles, Marx had examined the relationship between politics and economics, but he concluded that he lacked a deep knowledge for effective social criticism. To achieve that, he would need to investigate politics and economics (or political economy) in more detail.

MARX, PARIS, AND *THE ECONOMIC AND PHILOSOPHICAL MANUSCRIPTS*

Marx married Jenny von Westphalen (1814–1881) and moved to Paris in October 1843. The French capital exerted a profound influence on both of them. The French novelist Honoré de Balzac (1799–1850) paints Paris as a 'monstrous miracle, an astounding assemblage of movements, machines and ideas, the city of a thousand different romances, the world's thinking-box' (Balzac, 1972, 33). Paris was filled with artists, intellectuals, and revolutionaries, who were either publishing books, writing poetry, or conversing in cafes. Paris was also home to a large class of Germany émigrés, and Marx became friends with the German poet Heinrich Heine (1797–1856). Political agitation and social ferment were in the air, and Marx was quickly caught up in the talk of communism and revolution.

The Economic and Philosophical Manuscripts (the 'Paris Manuscripts') were written between April and August 1844. They were not published until after Marx's death in 1883, albeit in a severely edited form. The key ideas of the manuscripts – alienation, labour, private property, and communism – make up Marx's humanism. Unlike *Capital*, which will be discussed in Chapter Four, these texts focus more on the individual worker than on economic structures. They are an important text for those who wish to emphasise Marx's commitment to humanist ideas.

HUMANISM

Humanism is a branch of philosophy that empathises the value and agency of human beings, either individually or collectively. It became prominent during the Renaissance, when European scholars rediscovered classical Greek and Latin texts; then again during the Enlightenment in the eighteenth century. Across these different historical periods, humanism has tended to focus on human dignity, beauty, ability, and potential. Marxists differ on the extent and nature of Marx's humanism. Philosophers such as Louis Althusser (1918–1990) argue that humanism was simply a stage that Marx passed through before uncovering the science of society in *Capital*. For others, such as Marshall Berman (1940–2013), Marx was a radical intently concerned with human freedom and human flourishing, and was a fierce opponent of capitalism precisely because of the damaging effect it had on the individual.

Marx begins with a discussion of political economy, covering topics including wages, labour, profits, rents, and the relations between capitalists. He criticises the work of the political economists David Ricardo (1772–1823) and Adam Smith

(1723–1790). The Paris Manuscripts are Marx's correction of political economy, where he focuses on the condition of workers under capitalism, showing them to be torn apart by capitalist social relations. They are not a finished work, but reveal a process of development, refinement, and clarification as Marx develops critical accounts of alienation, capital, and communism. Marx proposes a rich philosophical humanism which seeks to achieve human freedom by transcending economic systems that perpetuate the exploitation of workers. The Paris Manuscripts have missing pages and difficult prose, but they remain a captivating work, a powerful sketch that would be refined over the next two decades. In Paris, Marx's thought underwent a decisive shift. He became convinced that 'philosophy could not solve' these problems alone (Marx, *MECW3*, 302). The world could only be changed through political struggle. In Paris, Marx became a communist.

FRIEDRICH ENGELS (1820–1895)

Engels was a lifelong friend of Marx, but he made distinguished contributions of his own and was one of the most prominent intellectuals of the nineteenth century. The son of a German manufacturer, Engels possessed excellent knowledge of commerce, industry, and the working class. He turned to communism and revolution after witnessing the greed, cunning, violence, 'hypocrisy, inconsistency and immorality' of capital (Engels, *MECW3*, 420). His 1844 article 'Outlines of the Critique of Political Economy' (*MECW3*, 375) pushed Marx to consider the work of the political economists in greater detail. In *The Condition of the Working Class in England* (1844), Engels gave a detailed exposition of the squalid, filthy conditions of factories and their surrounding districts. His *Anti-Dühring* (1877) was the first book to publicise Marxism to the German working classes. The scientific basis of Marxism was expounded in *Dialectics of Nature* (1883), a text not published until 1927. Engels has been positioned as responsible for the development of Marx's work into Marxism. He did ultimately synthesise Marx's philosophical achievements into core tenets, such as historical materialism, dialectical materialism, and scientific Marxism.

THE GERMAN IDEOLOGY

Marx's next text was written with Friedrich Engels. Now called *The German Ideology* (the original had no title), it was written mainly in Brussels, from 1845–46, although not published until 1932. Criticism and critique were Marx's lifeblood and he conceived of this text as a detailed examination of the current state of German philosophy, criticising three major figures of idealism: Ludwig Feuerbach (1804–1872), Bruno Bauer (1809–1882), and Max Stirner (1806–1856).

Marx first wrote a basic outline for the book, the 'Theses on Feuerbach', a series of 11 philosophical propositions on the importance of materialism and practical activity (in contrast to the idealism of the above thinkers). Engels discovered these tucked away in a notebook, and edited and published them as an appendix in his own book, *Ludwig Feuerbach and the End of German Classical Philosophy* (1888). The eleventh thesis is the most famous, compelling in its call for political action: 'the philosophers have only *interpreted* the world in various ways; the point however is to *change* it' (Marx, *MECW5*, 5). For Marx, philosophy should inspire real, practical activity.

The German Ideology is a baggy, 'genre-bending' text (Kornbluh, 2019, 21). It incorporates 'essays, manifestos, declarations of philosophical tenets, logical equations, sustained jokes, lists of maxims, uninterrupted catalogues of uninterpreted quotations, shorthand notes for future elucidation, gnomic slogans unadorned and play-written scripts for the dramas that might take place' (*ibid.*, 21). In it, Marx and Engels tried to provide a critique of ideology and a manifesto for a materialist method. Marx's aim was 'to settle accounts with our former philosophical conscience [...] in the form of a critique of post-Hegelian philosophy' and to formulate a political alternative (Marx and Engels, 1998). The current text of the *The German Ideology* covers some 500 pages over two volumes. It was never published in Marx's lifetime, and was rejected for publication several times. The most important part of it is the section on Feuerbach. Marx argued that Feuerbach's conception of humanity was idealist, remote from real social relations. For materialists, humans were the products of their environment.

But Marx went further. The economic realm, the forces and relations of material production, were crucial to shaping human behaviour. To understand this better, Marx formulated a new concept: the mode of production. For Marx, the 'the mode of production must not be considered simply as being the production of the physical existence of the individuals. Rather it is a definite form of activity of these individuals, a definite form of expressing their life, a definite mode of life on their part' (Marx, *MECW5*, 31). Social and political power, legal and religious power all flowed from property ownership. 'The nature of individuals thus depends on the material conditions determining their production' (Marx, *MECW5*, 31).

Focusing on production marked a major development in Marx's thought. *The German Ideology* shows the movement from the alienation of the Paris Manuscripts to a stronger focus on production, history, and class. For Marx, it was the development of the productive forces of society, coupled with capacity of workers to free themselves from alienating institutional structures, such as private property and religion, that would create a post-capitalist world. This provided a new basis for class, and class struggle, and would lead to one of the most popular and influential texts ever written: the *Communist Manifesto*. I discuss this text in Chapter Three. Only a small section of *The German Ideology* found its way into print, and the pressure of other projects proved far greater. Marx eventually abandoned the text to the 'gnawing criticism of the mice', claiming its chief purpose was self-clarification (Marx, *MECW29*, 264). Like the *The Economic and Philosophical Manuscripts*, it was not published until after Marx's death. The richness of the text resides more in suggestiveness than solution.

HISTORICAL MATERIALISM

It was Engels, not Marx, who put forward 'historical materialism' or the 'materialist conception of history'. This idea stresses a social–scientific understanding of historical development, which, as Engels writes, refers to 'that view of the course of history which seeks the ultimate cause and the great moving power of all important historic events in the economic development of society, in the changes in the modes of production and exchange, in the consequent division of society into distinct classes, and in the struggle of the these classes against one another' (Engels, *MECW27*, 304). This doctrine can be traced to two influential texts written by Engels: *Anti-Dühring* (1877), a part of which later became *Socialism: Utopian and Scientific* (1880); and *Dialectics of Nature* (1883). While there is far more theoretical richness to these texts than is typically granted, Engels' 'mechanical materialism' differs sharply from Marx's own formulations.

LONDON

Marx arrived in London in 1849. It was here, over a period of some 20 years, that he wrote *Capital*, spending long hours researching and writing in the Reading Room of the British Museum. He later became involved with the International Workingmen's Association, a political organisation of workers, trade unionists, and socialists. Marx had wanted to concentrate on *Capital* and had declined requests to participate in political groups. But, nearing completion of his work, he wished to return to politics. He accepted the invitation and, by the end of the evening, was on the General Council.

INTERNATIONAL WORKINGMEN'S ASSOCIATION

Founded in London on 28th September 1864, 'the International' was a political organisation that attempted to unite left-wing socialist, communist, and anarchist groups that were engaged in working class activities and class struggle. Marx was invited to attend the evening by a French radical and later wrote the inaugural address, which stated the ultimate aim of the IWA to be the 'abolition of all class rule'. Marx mainly worked on issues of strategy and coordination, seeking to unite the various European organisations. By the 1870s, Marx was the leading figure of the IWA.

FINAL YEARS

Marx's final years were plagued by ill health The Marx family had lived in near squalor in London, with little to eat, sometimes with eight people sharing two small rooms. Marx even wrote of his inability to leave the house on some days because his coat and shoes were in the pawnshop. Marx learned about the intricacies of capital through his reading in the British Museum, but he learned about the domestic life of the working class through gruesome first-hand experience (Stallybrass, 1998, 191). The death of Marx's children (one child dying before they could be named) were all profound losses. In an 1855 letter to Engels, he describes the condition of the household after the recent death of his son:

> The house is naturally quite desolate and forlorn since the death of the dear child who was its life and soul. The way we miss him at every turn is quite indescribable. I have been through all kinds of misfortune in my time, but it is only now that I know what real unhappiness is. I feel myself broken down. It is a good thing that since the day of the burial I have had such furious headaches that I cannot think or see or hear. In all the terrible agonies I have experienced these days, the thought of you and your friendship has always sustained me, and the hope that, together, we may still do something sensible in the world.
>
> (Marx, *MECW39*, 533).

Marx continued working, and became interested in Russia. He had planned to write a clarification, after he had been asked by a Russian periodical, on whether Russia – a poor country with little industry – need follow the lines of Western economic development. He did not complete this text, but left behind thousands of pages of manuscript. Marx died on 14th March 1883 and was buried in Highgate Cemetery. Engels gave the farewell address, comparing his friend's achievements to those of Charles Darwin (1809–1882). Already, Engels can be seen to be establishing a specific reading of Marx's work and acting as a decisive agent in the struggle for Marx's system. The battle of interpretations had begun. I will examine this in the 'After Marx' section.

SUMMARY

Marx lived an eventful life. After university, he went into journalism and became editor of the Cologne newspaper, the *Rheinische Zeitung*. Marx then moved to Paris, where he became a communist and studied political economy. In *The Economic and Philosophical Manuscripts*, Marx knew that the work of political economists did not consider the real material existence of the workers. He realised that capitalism was a system that alienated workers from the product of their labour, and only through the abolition of private property could alienation be ended. In *The German Ideology*, Marx turned to production, history, and class. This critique of German philosophy started with 'real individuals, their activity, and the material conditions of their life' (Marx, *MECW5*, 31). Moving to London in 1849, Marx began his research in the Reading Room of the British Museum, culminating 18 years later in his magnum opus *Capital*. In the 1860s and 1870s, Marx returned to political activity through his involvement with the International Workingmen's Association. He died in 1883.

2

SOURCES OF IDEAS

The most important source for Marx was G.W.F. Hegel (1770–1831). For Marx, Hegel brings a unique intellectual voice, a range of powerful concepts, and a will to question traditional thought. Marx approaches (and sometimes appropriates) Hegel's key ideas for his own critique of capitalism, while also criticising Hegel in turn. An understanding of Hegel is important to be able to fully understand Marx. In this chapter I will introduce Hegel's ideas and explain two key concepts essential for Marx: totality and dialectic.

DIALECTIC

Dialectic has held a central place in Western philosophical systems since Plato. In the most general sense, dialectic is a process of social or conceptual discord in which the staging of the conflict of oppositions leads to a fuller or more adequate mode of perception or thought. The word 'dialectic' derives from the Greek and means 'to converse'. It involves a process whereby two opposing arguments or positions are 'solved' by a third one. The first position, the thesis, is followed by the antithesis and both are resolved in a synthesis. In turn, the synthesis becomes the conceptual starting point for a further logical argument. Crucially, the dialectic is constantly unfolding and is never complete in any traditional sense.

For Marx, the final stage of the dialectic is the creation of communism.

Hegel is a difficult philosopher. As one academic jokes, reading Hegel 'is often a trying and exhausting experience, the equivalent of chewing gravel' (Beiser, 2005, 1). But Hegel wanted to be difficult. He often talked of the labour of intellectual thought, the superficiality of common sense, and the strenuous efforts of philosophical insight. I could begin with an anecdote, but Hegel hated them. An anecdote is a detached incident or a funny event that gives a brief, revealing account. For Hegel, no matter how striking or interesting, anecdotes were not philosophy. Philosophy was a search for truth, a set of arguments about the world. Any amusing story, thought Hegel, is always partial and incomplete. It is part of a bigger truth, and that truth, no matter what it may be, is always more important.

This tells us something important about Hegel's philosophy. He was interested in the whole or the *totality* (the world taken all together). For Hegel, only the whole was true. This totality is the product of a process that preserves all of its moments as elements in a structure. The totality is always moving, meaning it cannot be described in a linear way. Many Marxist literary critics, such as Georg Lukács (1885–1971) and Fredric Jameson (1934–), have been interested in the relationship between totality and literature, suggesting that the narrative space of the novel, for instance, presents a kind of totality. As the totality is always in flux and movement, Hegel (and Marx) use a form of philosophical argument called dialectic. Before detailing these two ideas, I will first introduce Hegel.

THE PHENOMENOLOGY OF SPIRIT (1807)

This is Hegel's most discussed work, and also one of the most important books in western philosophy. With its publication, Hegel moved from being an unknown academic to a world-celebrated philosopher. Hegel famously – and rather grandly – described the *Phenomenology* to his students as a 'voyage of discovery', leading some scholars to refer to the text as a kind of instruction manual or '*Bildung*' of consciousness (Pinkard, in Hegel, 2018, xli). The book charts a movement from a naïve empiricism (knowing only what our senses tell us) to what Hegel calls 'Absolute Spirit' ('a certainty of unconditional self-knowing'). In this sense, the book is not philosophy but a preparation for philosophy, a series of concepts and categories that the individual must work through. This movement towards self-consciousness is dialectical insofar as every stage develops into the next through a process of contradiction, negating the previous stage while preserving something of it, a process Hegel called '*Aufhebung*' (to lift up, abolish, or transcend).

G.W.F. HEGEL

Hegel was born in Stuttgart in 1770. His father was a senior financial official in the administration of Württemberg, and Hegel's mother tutored him in Latin before he attended school. He was a precocious child and kept a journal, copying out long extracts from the books that he read. Hegel was born at a time when German intellectual culture and European history were moving from romanticism to modernism.

MODERNISM

Modernism is an artistic movement that lasted from the nineteenth century to the end of the Second World War (1939–1945), but was particularly prominent in the years following the First World War. In art, modernist movements included cubism, futurism, vorticism, and surrealism. These movements reflected the experience of human subjects in relation to new and rapidly developing technologies, such as the car, radio, telephone, and film. For example, cubism fractures or shatters traditional forms to show an increasingly fragile and chaotic world, while surrealism juxtaposes uncommon images (like melting watches) to challenge a division between dream and reality. Sigmund Freud's theories of psychoanalysis proved influential, while in literature, authors explored interior subjectivity with techniques such as interior monologue and stream of consciousness. Key works by T.S. Eliot (*The Waste Land*, 1922), Gertrude Stein (*Tender Buttons*, 1914), James Joyce (*Ulysses*, 1922), Virginia Woolf (*Mrs Dalloway*, 1925), and John Dos Passos (*U.S.A.*, 1938), among others, constituted the new art of this age.

This period was one of dramatic change. During Hegel's life, monarchies crumbled, the shock waves of revolution emanated from France and America, and rapid changes in industry and technology were initiating a movement towards economic globalisation. Hegel was prompted to reflect on human subjectivity, on ideas of individuality and self-realisation, and on the other hand, the importance of the community and the collective. By the time of his death in 1831, Hegel and his generation had witnessed some of the most stunning and sustained changes that have ever occurred. As a philosopher, Hegel tried to comprehend these vast changes, circumstances, and experiences, attempting to give shape and clarity to the momentous events and experiences of his generation. His writings 'can be explained by the need to come to terms with the painful, perturbing, conflict-ridden moral experience of the world of the French Revolution' (Taylor, 1975, 3). Hegel, then, is the first philosopher to make 'modernity itself the subject of his thought' (Pinkad, 2001, x).

The concepts and categories developed by Hegel were essential for Marx. Hegel produced four major philosophical works during his lifetime, but *The Phenomenology of Spirit* (1807) is his most influential. The *Phenomenology* is a kind of instruction manual – or a 'ladder of forms' – that Hegel believes each individual must work through before they can begin to do philosophy. In this work, Hegel created a comprehensive, systematic, and dialectical philosophy that proposed a teleological account of history (teleology means explaining things in relation to their purpose, end, or goal). Marx famously 'inverted' Hegel's idealism into a materialist theory that culminated in communism. While

Hegel was a conservative, and Marx was a revolutionary, both thinkers nevertheless share an interest in dialectic.

The starting point for Hegel was idealism, the world of spirit or self-conscious reason. According to Hegel, our consciousness is alienated from itself, and it cannot understand its own true nature. In order to realise its own true nature, consciousness needs to develop 'Absolute Knowing' (Hegel, 1977, 479). For Hegel, then, alienation was a matter of the spirit, a failure to achieve a recognition of belonging within a community. Overcoming alienation was a matter of self-discovery and the development of an absolute knowledge (the self-development of the human being). Marx was far more attuned to economic realities, showing in *The Economic and Philosophical Manuscripts* that alienation was the direct result of capitalist social relations and the misery of the working class.

The most important passage in the *Phenomenology* is the master/slave section. Here, Hegel is dealing with self-consciousness, arguing that the human subject can be recognised only through another human subject. A problem or contradiction arises when this occurs between individuals. 'The Master demands recognition from the slave while also refusing recognition of the slave as even having the status to confer such recognition at all' (Pinkard, in Hegel, 2018, xxiii) The master, then, requires recognition from somebody else: someone authorised to bestow such recognition. On the other hand, the slave, in working for the master, acquires a self-consciousness over and above the domineering master. The subject recognises the identity of the master, while the master does not recognise their own identity, or that of the subject. It is work that transforms the slave into a fully developed, mature, self-conscious individual.

HEGEL'S DIALECTIC

Hegel's dialectic is a voracious, totalising, all-consuming thing (Lane, 2008, 12). It is a mode of argument, but I want to stress here that it is the qualities of perception that dominate, and that make Hegel's version of the dialectic such a vital and fascinating system. Indeed, the argument *is* the dialectical movement, which is restless and ever in flux, much like capitalism itself. Many postmodern thinkers, such as Jean Baudrillard (1929–2007), have critiqued the totalising aspects of Hegel's dialectic, claiming (with some justification) that there are experiences which remain immune to dialectical thought procedures. In recent years, there have been some powerful reassessments of Hegel's dialectic that concentrate on, to use a musical theme, the many variations of his system. As a mode of argument, it is also a way of perceiving the problem. It involves the clash of two opposing concepts that come together to generate a solution. The most important part of dialectic is that it is attuned to change, movement, and transformation. David Harvey gives a good example. Children, Harvey argues, are cannily dialectical: they see everything in flux, in motion. They see connections between seemingly separate objects, contradictions, and changes. For them, the world moves. In contrast, adults tend to prefer fixed or static categories. For Harvey, the 'better trained you are in a discipline, the less used to dialectical method you're likely to be' (Harvey, 2010, 13). Marx uses dialectic to grasp dynamic changes and processes. In a word, dialectic reveals motion.

Hegel gives examples of dialectic, but he also *writes* dialectically. When Hegel says 'the whole is the true', he means that truth does not always reveal itself at the beginning (Hegel, 2018). Rather than rush to a result, which we are all eager to do, we need to think carefully about the whole process. 'This is so because the subject matter is not exhausted in its aims; rather, it is exhaustively treated when it is worked out. Nor is the result which is reached the actual whole itself; rather, the whole is the result together with the way the result comes to be' (Hegel, 2018, 5). This is a difficult quotation, and a good indication of the style in which Hegel writes. To make matters simpler, think of an acorn and an oak tree, an example Hegel himself uses. The two are separate, but the acorn contains potential (it will one day grow into a mighty oak tree), and the oak tree contains history (it was once the little acorn). You need to wait for the acorn to become an oak tree to see the full process. This is why, argues Hegel, it is important to think in terms of the totality. Hegel's philosophy enlarges the arena of thought to see everything: change, transformation, and movement!

In his work, Hegel develops a dialectic dealing with contradiction, unity, and opposites. Hegel's philosophy had a conservative and a radical side. As a member of the Doctor's Club, Marx was also, for a time, a Young Hegelian. This was a group of German thinkers engaged in radical critiques of Hegel's philosophy. Hegel believed he was living in the end of history: a postrevolutionary moment, or the close of the historical dynamic, where conflict had ended and individual subjects had attained freedom and democracy. For Hegel, spirit (*Geist*) was the animating force of historical development. Marx rejected this theological standpoint, choosing to champion social classes and the forces of production as agents of change. For Marx, Hegel had failed to explore the essential connection between philosophy and the oppressive, exploitative, and inhuman nature of capitalism. But Hegel had a lasting influence on Marx's economic theory, with Marx constructing his critique of political economy in relation to Hegel's use of dialectical concepts and procedures. In the afterword to *Capital*, which I will discuss in Chapter Four, Marx represents this as an inversion, claiming:

> My dialectic method is, in its foundations, not only different from the Hegelian, but exactly opposite to it. For Hegel, the process of thinking, which he even transforms into an independent subject, under the name of 'the Idea', is the creator of the real world, and the real world is only the external appearance of the idea. With me the reverse is true: the ideal is nothing but the material world reflected in the mind of man, and translated into forms of thought.

> (Marx, 1990, 102)

Marx uses dialectic to understand how capitalism moves, to see how everything is in process, in motion. Marx talks about processes, about the capitalist mode of production, not about capital as a static thing.

The relation between Hegel and Marx is an important and complicated one, with Marx often concealing and obscuring his debt to Hegel. While Marx acknowledges the Hegelian dialectic 'is what separates his work from [...] mainstream bourgeois thought', Marx is complicit in constructing 'the myth of Hegel the idealist who had everything upside down' (MacGregor,

2015, 11). In the narrowest sense, then, Marx uses Hegel's dialectic as a method of negation, enabling him to observe the process by which categories arise from Hegel to form more inclusive totalities, which he makes the starting point of his own research. Marx developed his own stunning, innovative works, but Hegel remained a vital presence for Marx.

As I argued in Chapter One, Marx began studying political economy seriously in 1843, after writing a critique of Hegel's philosophy. Hegel defended landed estates, property, and monarchy. For Marx, Hegel failed to grasp the specificity of empirical occurrences, turned away from human subjects, and mistakenly aligned individual interest with state interest. But it is inaccurate to argue that Marx rejected Hegel, or simply sought to replace Hegel's approach with an economic analysis of private property. It was Marx's attention to the powers and pleasures of Hegel's prose that transformed Marx's writings into a series of critical positions. Marx challenged Hegel, while at the same time preserving and developing his work at a higher conceptual level, which is the core of dialectic.

TOTALITY

Hegel's other major idea is totality. The totality is a developmental process made up of individual moments. The sum of these moments is the complete structure. Marx inherits the idea of totality from Hegel and tries, in *Capital*, to give a picture of capitalism as a process of connected categories. For Georg Lukács, the use of totality is the distinctive feature of Marx's thought. 'The category of totality, the all-pervasive supremacy of the whole over the parts is the essence of the method which Marx took over from Hegel and brilliantly transformed into the foundations of a wholly new science' (Lukács, 1971, 27). The key issue here is how to present the totality? For both Marx and Hegel, this necessitates the use of a dialectical method, one of the few types of argument that can comprehend society in flux, movement, and change.

SUMMARY

Hegel was an immensely important philosopher for Marx. Hegel was an idealist and believed in the world of spirit (*Geist*), or self-conscious reason, as the animating force of hsitory. *The Phenomenology of Spirit* is his most important and influential work. Hegel proposes a movement from a naïve empiricism (knowing only what our senses represent to us) to absolute knowledge (taken to be a true knowledge of the mind's own nature). Hegel's philosophy had a conservative and a radical side. He defended monarchy, private property, and inheritance; but the Young Hegelians, of which Marx was once a member, drew radical conclusions from Hegel's work, arguing that it showed an obvious need for social and political reform of the German state. In particular, Marx adopted from Hegel two key concepts which he would use throughout his own work: dialectic and totality. While Hegel was an idealist thinker who supported conservative politics, Marx was a materialist committed to social revolution and communism.

3

THE *COMMUNIST MANIFESTO*

The key message of the *Manifesto* is communist revolution, urging the workers of all countries to unite and overthrow the capitalist class. It was this focus on the necessity of social change that made Marx different from other left-wing political groups. Marx's communism was more radical: it proposed class struggle, revolution, and the abolition of private property. Published in London in 1848, the *Manifesto* is one of Marx's early works (written when he was 29 years old), yet it captures many of his key ideas – on class, capital, communism, and revolution. In this chapter, I will unpack Marx's text and show how the *Manifesto* contains some of his most important concepts.

The *Manifesto* is a work of striking elegance and precision. Marx had to convey the importance of communism in the most clear and simple manner. It is very short, but packed with stunning images. It appeared ahead of the revolutions and political upheavals that took place throughout Europe in 1848, in France, Austria, Poland, Italy, and Germany, but went largely unnoticed until the 1870s. While living in Brussels, Marx had been corresponding with a group of communists living in London. The London communists were impressed with Marx and asked him to write the *Manifesto*. They had already given him drafts, and his task was now to write a new document combining a solid theoretical foundation with a strong political exhortation.

Marx begins with a ghost: 'A spectre is haunting Europe – the spectre of Communism' (Marx, 2019, 61). 'All the old powers of Europe have entered into a holy alliance to exorcise this spectre' (Marx, 2019, 61). Capitalism, Marx argues, is haunted by the possibility of a different kind of existence: a radical, more egalitarian form of social and economic production called communism. Marx's invocation of the ghost is important. Ghosts are complex temporal entities. They are figures of the past, who return in the present, to change the future. This is why Marx's spectre points forward and backward; forward in its call for revolutionary action; backward in the sense of Marx acknowledging just how this revolutionary point was reached. This ghost is an example of how Marx uses gothic literary tropes to show capitalism is haunted by the possibility of a non-capitalist world.

Importantly, the ghost shows that communism was conjured by capital. It was immanent, already there in the social relation. Marx is making it clear that he did not invent communism; rather, it was called into existence as the opposing force to capital. For Marx, the ghost is perceived as threatening because communism is 'acknowledged by all European powers to be itself a power (Marx, 2019, 61). More importantly however, the arrival of the ghost marks the moment when communists 'should openly, in the face of the whole world, publish their views, their aims, their tendencies, and meet this [...] Spectre of Communism with a manifesto of the party itself' (Marx, 2019, 61). For communists, the ghost was a cause of celebration, not a gothic terror.

BOURGEOISIE AND PROLETARIAT

The central characters of the *Manifesto* are the bourgeoisie and the proletariat, locked in epic struggle. This is the first part of the *Manifesto*. To read this section is to be confronted with a frank admission that appears paradoxical. Marx begins by praising the bourgeoisie, who have 'played a most revolutionary part' (Marx, 2019, 64). Why does Marx do this? Has he not come to overthrow the bourgeoisie and champion the working class? This is because, for Marx, the achievements of the bourgeoisie rival all the great civilisations of the past. They have been the 'first to show what man's activity can bring about', accomplishing 'wonders far surpassing Egyptian pyramids, Roman aqueducts, and Gothic cathedrals' (Marx, 2019, 64). These accomplishments are the mills, factories, roads, bridges, telegraphs, and canals – but also the immense movements of people to new cities and continents. Under the bourgeoisie, small towns had exploded into sprawling, thriving, and bustling industrial and commercial centres. But these migrations to new places and spaces were always inspired, and brutally enforced, in the search for greater profit. For Marx, the bourgeoisie, more than any other class in history, had revolutionised the forces and relations of production.

In this opening section, Marx's interest is in the world-transforming energies of the bourgeoisie, but he wants to show how this has occurred. In earlier periods, there was 'a complicated arrangement of society into various orders, a manifold gradation of social rank (Marx, 2019, 62). Marx gives examples from Ancient Rome (patricians, plebeians, slaves) and the Middle Ages (feudal lords, apprentices, serfs) which make up the gradations of social classes. Importantly, the bourgeoisie has not done away with class distinctions – Marx uses the term 'antagonisms', which is more confrontational – but has 'established new classes, new conditions of oppression, new forms of struggle' (Marx, 2019, 62). For Marx, the achievements of the bourgeoisie should not blind us to the oppressions created by this class.

Crucially, the bourgeoisie has one distinctive feature over all other classes. It has 'simplified the class antagonisms' (Marx, 2019, 62). Where once there were many classes, now there are just two. For Marx, 'Society as a whole is more and more splitting up into two great hostile camps, into two great classes directly facing each other: bourgeoise and proletariat' (Marx, 2019, 62). This is Marx's view of the world in the *Manifesto*, and it leads to one of his most prophetic statements: the 'history of all hitherto existing society is the history of class struggles' (Marx, 2019, 61). The basic point being made here is that the struggle between different and opposing classes, determined by their relation in a mode of production, is central to both understanding and transforming the world. Marx has now cleared the ground for his communist politics. Class struggle, leading to revolution, is the most important task of communism.

The final part of this section describes the implications of capitalist production. This story is told through a series of rapid-fire images. The needs of the world market 'chases the bourgeoise over the whole surface of the globe' (Marx, 2019, 65). Human wants, desires, and tastes are remade. The 'exploitation of the world market' has 'given a cosmopolitan character' to every country (Marx, 2019, 65). Modern networks of production, communication, and exchange have battered down old national alignments like heavy artillery. Marx's snapshots succeed one another and blend together 'with a reckless momentum, a breathless intensity' (Berman, 2002, 91). This flash of succeeding images is presented dialectically, where each new development emerges out of the old. Marx describes the movement of capitalism as both positive and negative, asking us to grasp all these complex tensions in a single breath or sentence. He insists on the truly revolutionary nature of capitalism, which is engaged in a process of expansion that will consume the globe.

Marx charts the horrors and adventures of modernity in a 'lyrical celebration of bourgeoise works' (Berman, 2002, 15). The bourgeoisie have swept everything before them, have 'drowned the most heavenly ecstasies of religious fervour, of chivalrous enthusiasm, of philistine sentimentalism, in the icy waters of egotistical calculation (Marx, 2019, 65). They have 'left remaining no other nexus between man and man than naked self-interest, than callous "cash payment"' (Marx, 2019, 64). Everyone is reduced to what they can pay or earn, to their cash value. Personal worth has become exchange value: 'in place of the numberless indefeasible chartered freedoms' the bourgeoisie has 'set up that single, unconscionable freedom – Free Trade' (Marx, 2019, 64). Exploitation has grown worse: 'In one word, for exploitation, veiled by religious and political illusions, it has substituted naked, shameless, direct, *brutal* exploitation' (Marx, 2019, 64, my italics). Great professions of culture and learning – the 'physician, the lawyer, the priest, the poet, the man of science' – have all been converted into 'paid wage labourers' (Marx, 2019, 64). For Marx, capitalism robs humanity of its essence, turning social existence into a 'mere money relation' (Marx, 2019, 64). All other kinds of value are subordinated to this standard. In the world of the bourgeoisie, cash is king.

Capitalism may have conquered the world, but it is also a self-destructive force. For Marx, impermanence is the very condition of its existence. It is an economic mode where 'all that is solid melts into air' (Marx, 2019, 64). Marx's metaphor captures the contradictions of capitalism; it is an 'environment that promises us adventure, power, joy growth, transformation of ourselves and the world – and, at the same time, that threatens to destroy everything we have, everything we know, everything we are'; it is 'a paradoxical unity, a unity of disunity [...] a maelstrom of perpetual disintegration and renewal, of struggle and contradiction, of ambiguity and anguish (Berman, 2002, 15). Marx wishes to impress upon us the complexity and richness of nineteenth-century capitalism in all its spectacle and horror. For everything to 'melt' means for Marx, and many other modernists, to embrace the world's potentialities while fighting against its most palpable tyrannies.

It is here that Marx wants to show how capitalism has moved beyond the powers of any single individual class. A central theme of Marx's description of capitalism is the ceaseless destruction of the old and the creation of the new. The collapse of old productive forces gives way to the conquest of new markets. For the bourgeoisie, creation and destruction go hand in hand. Crucially, the bourgeoisie is itself changing. Marx explains this metamorphosis through fantastical imagery, arguing that 'a society that has conjured up such gigantic means of production and of exchange, is like the sorcerer, who is no longer able to control the powers of nether world whom he has called up by his spells' (Marx, 2019, 8). Marx probably has in mind here the poem 'The Sorcerer's Apprentice' (1797) by Johann Wolfgang von Goethe (1749–1832), but with a subtle variation. In the original fairy tale, an apprentice enchants a broom to do his chores for him. He cannot stop the broom, and each time he splits it with an axe the pieces become whole and work at twice the speed. When all seems lost, the sorcerer returns and quickly breaks the spell, stopping the chaos. In Marx's version, the sorcerer – a symbol of the bourgeoisie – has no enchantment to stop the spread of capitalism and is overwhelmed by the very forces he has conjured. For Marx, the bourgeoise have called into existence the very class – the working class, or proletarians – that will overthrow them.

The spell of capitalism is now fully out of control. As industrial society had compelled men, women, and children into the mills and factories, it had created a new, unstoppable force. For Marx, the bourgeoisie is the agent of its own destruction, it 'therefore, produces, above all, its own grave-diggers' (Marx, 1998, 16).

PROLETARIANS AND COMMUNISTS

The second section of the *Manifesto* argues that the communists are the party of the working class. 'They have no interests separate and apart from those of the proletariat as a whole' (Marx, 2019, 73). Marx stakes a claim of originality here: the communists are different from other working-class parties because they are international. They 'point out and bring to the front the common interests of the entire proletariat, independently of all nationality' (Marx, 2019, 73). This broad focus means, at least for Marx, that the communists 'always and everywhere represent the interests of the movement as a whole' (Marx, 2019, 73). But if, for Marx, the communists are more advanced than other working-class parties, their aim is the same: the 'formation of the proletariat into a class, overthrow of the bourgeois supremacy, conquest of political power by the proletariat' (Marx, 2019, 74). If it appears that Marx is too sweeping in his comments, then this is because his aim is strategic: he is attempting to unify the working class behind a single set of principles and direct them towards revolutionary activity.

It is here that Marx puts forward the principles of the party. This consists of ten points, which include a call for the abolition of private property, the abolition of the right to inheritance, and an end to children working in factories. On the issue of nature and the natural world, the communists call for the enrichment of the soil and the cultivation of all waste lands. A clear social vision is presented in which classes are abolished and the 'free development of each is the condition for the free development of all' (Marx, 2019, 81). As Marx makes clear, communism is a social and economic relation that places freedom above profit. It calls for common ownership of the means of production. 'The theory of the Communists', Marx writes, 'may be summed up in the single sentence: Abolition of private property' (Marx, 2019,

74). This is crucial: communists must end 'modern bourgeoisie private property' because it is the 'most complete expression of the system of producing and appropriating products, that is based on class antagonisms, on the exploitation of the many by the few' (Marx, 2019, 74).

To illustrate this, Marx moves to political economy. As I argued in Chapter 1, Marx had started to think about the relationship between politics and economics in his articles for the Cologne newspaper and in *The Economic and Philosophic Manuscripts*. The *Manifesto* presents these ideas in a very simple format. In this sense, the *Manifesto*, like every other text that Marx wrote, builds upon his other work to date, showing a constant process of development and clarification as Marx refined his ideas.

Private property creates alienation because it robs the worker of the product of their labour and gives it to the capitalist. Marx is not talking about getting rid of 'Hard-won, self-acquired, self-earned property' (Marx, 2019, 74). The 'fruit of a man's own labour' which is the 'work of all personal freedom, activity, and independence' is rightfully yours. Nor is he talking about the ownership of everyday items. What Marx means is 'modern bourgeoise private property': the ownership of the means of production and access to the means of subsistence, as these determine the constitution of society. By getting rid of private property, the bourgeoisie cannot compel the proletariat to work for them. As such, in a communist society, one would not have to labour to live. Labour would be a 'means to widen, to enrich, to promote the existence of the labourer' rather than line the pockets of the capitalists (Marx, 2019, 75).

The most exciting aspect of communism is its potential. For Marx, communism is the path to freedom, but it is only a beginning. In a free society, no-one is any longer tied to the necessity of difficult daily labour. Humanity would have the time, the energy, and the will to pursue new modes of social existence. For Marx, communism involves 'the most radical rupture with traditional ideas' (Marx, 2019, 80). This is why it is so hard to grasp. Ideas for Marx are anchored in material life. 'Man's ideas, views, and conceptions, in a word, man's conciseness, changes with every change in the conditions of his material existence, in his social relations' (Marx, 2019, 79). Consider a world, Marx suggests, which makes routine the exercise of human capacities, potential-ities, and pleasures, barely imaginable in the cramped conditions of the present. That world, Marx reflects, would be truly rich, and worth fighting for. One can certainly take issue with Marx's ideas, but his desire to promote the well-being of humanity is certainly not in doubt.

SOCIALIST AND COMMUNIST LITERATURE

In the third section of the *Manifesto*, Marx offers a critique of other forms of socialism. He examines the pamphlets of French and German socialist and communist parties – the Reactionary Socialists, the Conservative Socialists, and the Utopian Socialists – taking them to task for their theoretical failures. Each approach fails, argues Marx, because it lacks a key component of communist theory: the Reactionaries fail to account for the meteoric rise of the bourgeoisie (as Marx does in the opening section); the Conservative Socialists do not understand the inev-itability of class conflict and trust in piecemeal reforms for the working class, which for Marx do not go far enough; the Critical Socialists reject revolutionary action, hoping 'to attain their ends by peaceful means', which Marx considers naïve, thinking that the capitalists will never voluntarily give up their dominant pos-ition in society (Marx, 2019, 89).

For Marx, only communism can create real change. But he also makes another important point: under capitalism, ideas can circulate rapidly (he has already talked about the speed with which goods circulate the globe). For instance, when the socialist and communist literature of France was introduced to Germany, Marx points out that 'French social conditions had not immigrated along with them' (Marx, 2019, 85). Marx's point here is that ideas that worked in one situation cannot be simply picked up and deployed in an entirely different one. Ideas that are borrowed are often robbed of their theoretical significance. For Marx, one must consider the real, practical, material situ-ation of each country. For him, communism does exactly that. Communism is a political approach that is anchored in a deep study of the social and economic relations of capitalism.

THE POSITION OF THE COMMUNISTS

The final section of the *Manifesto* is very short, barely more than a page. It reflects clear compositional haste, and the pressures of the deadlines that were imposed on Marx by the London communists. He simply did not have time to finish it, although a short ending generally works in favour of a text like the *Manifesto*. Marx ends by trying to pull together the various strands of the document. 'In short', writes Marx, 'Communists everywhere support every revolutionary movement against the existing social and political order' (Marx, 2019, 92). The 'leading question', he reminds us, is the 'property question' (Marx, 2019, 92). Marx also wants to bridge any divides between other political parties. He argues that communists 'labour for the union and agreement of the democratic parties of all countries' (Marx, 2019, 92). It is a collective effort aimed at overcoming the structural exploitation of the workers under capitalism. The final few lines are among the most bold and memorable, with Marx returning to the gothic horror invoked at the very beginning. This time it is directed at the bourgeoisie: 'Let the ruling classes tremble at a communist revolution', Marx writes, 'The proletarians have nothing to lose but their chains. They have a world to win' (Marx, 2019, 94). The central message of the text is given in the final exhortation, in large bold letters: 'WORKING MEN OF ALL COUNTRIES, UNITE!' (Marx, 2019, 94). Only through a truly international focus – workers of the world – could communism be achieved.

In my discussion, I have shown how Marx's key ideas (on capital, communism, revolution, and political economy) are contained in this short document. They are not all fully developed – this would mean a much longer document – but they are apparent when we read the *Manifesto* carefully. However, it is important to note that Marx did not finish with them here. He spent his life developing his thoughts, and was constantly engaged in a process of reading, writing, and re-writing. In consequence, he would return to the *Manifesto* in later life. He and Engels wrote a new preface for the German edition in 1872. Marx managed another preface, this time for a Russian edition, one year before his death. While it is a document of its time, the intense vision of the *Manifesto* leaps forward in time to give a glimpse of a future beyond capitalism. It has become an enduring work of literature and philosophy and is perhaps the 'most revolutionary document ever given to the world' (Harney, *MECW39*, 60). The text was so incendiary that after its publication in 1848 by the London communists, the Belgian Government – alarmed by a popular revolt in France – gave Marx one day's notice to leave his home in Brussels and never return.

SUMMARY

The *Manifesto* is Marx's most popular and enduring work. Published in London shortly before revolutions and political upheavals throughout Europe in 1848, the text went largely unnoticed but powerfully captured the revolutionary sentiment of the time. The *Manifesto* sets out the principles and positions of the Communist Party, but it also gives a philosophically rich view of communism as a new social and economic relation committed to human freedom. In the *Manifesto*, Marx establishes a distinctly proletarian position that argues the working class can and should overturn capitalism through revolution. His descriptions of the path forged by industrial capitalism are rightly considered to be among the most stunning descriptions of the period, drenched in symbolism, metaphor, and allegory. Marx recognised the wealth-creating power of capitalism and accurately predicted that it would conquer the world, warning that this new form of globalisation would have dire and divisive consequences. The *Manifesto* turned out to be a prophetic text. It anticipates the scale and intensity of globalisation where market forces seemingly hold power over individuals. Importantly, Marx shows that communism is not opposed to working-class parties; communism is in the interest of all workers.

4

CAPITAL AND CAPITALISM

In Season 2 of *American Gods* (2017), adapted from Neil Gaiman's 2001 fantasy novel, Shadow and Mr Wednesday are sitting in a diner in St Louis. Shadow remarks that in 1933 President Franklin Delano Roosevelt (1882–1945) took the United States off the Gold Standard, meaning that you could no longer walk into a bank and redeem paper money for gold or silver:

> Shadow: You said money is the most powerful god in America. But money isn't worth anything.
>
> Wednesday: I have a piece of paper, hm? But I want this saltshaker. You have the saltshaker, but you're willing to take my piece of paper for your saltshaker. Now, why would you do that? Because this isn't actually a piece of paper; it's a story. And the story that you've heard over and over and over again. And it's been drummed into you that this is worth something. This is of value. No matter what country, culture, or religion. The whole world loves money. The greatest story ever told.

Marx tells the story of money in *Capital*. But money is only one small part of capitalism. Capitalism is a mode of production based on private ownership, capital accumulation, wage labour, and the extraction of surplus value from the worker, which is the 'amount by which the value of the product exceeds the value of its constituent elements' (Marx, 1990, 320). Capitalism embeds relations of domination and exploitation; hence a central feature is the antagonistic relation – the clash of opposing forces – between capitalists and workers, which Marx spelled out in the *Communist Manifesto*. *Capital* is concerned with the economic and political structure of capitalist society.

Marx explores capital from different critical standpoints. It 'is the ultimate aim of this work', he writes, 'to reveal the economic law of motion of modern society' (*ibid.*, 92). Over the rest of the book, Marx analyses the inner workings of the capitalist system, examining the commodity, money, capital, the production of surplus value, the working day, wages, machinery, technology, labour, theories of colonisation, and agriculture. It is a truly staggering work. Marx's analysis of capitalism is premised on the notion that the modes of organisation shaping history and society are constantly changing. This change derives from the interactions between the different levels, for instance between the level of technological development on one hand, and the division of labour on the other. These interactions are led by different social groups possessing different economic and political interests (Foley, 2019, 5). To account for this, Marx represents capitalism as a totality, which can only be described dialectically.

Money, for Marx, makes possible exchange between workers and capitalists, and the circulation of commodities. Money is not the cause of inequality, but a symptom of structural contradictions. Behind money, Marx discovers value, production, and capitalist power over labour. To understand how Marx reaches this conclusion, we need to begin with the simplest element of capitalism: the commodity.

THE COMMODITY

Marx kick-starts *Capital* with a discussion of commodities: 'The wealth of societies in which the capitalist mode of production prevails appears as an "immense collection of commodities"; the individual commodity appears as its elementary form. Our analysis therefore begins with an analysis of the commodity' (Marx, 1990, 125). The commodity – whether a smartphone, a pair of shoes, or a pizza – is a good or service produced for the purpose of exchange, separate from, and not belonging to, the person who made it (in capitalist societies we sell our labour for wages to buy what we need, no matter how widely we might define these needs). The production of goods and services has existed in every society, otherwise its members would not survive. But there is something special about commodity production. 'The whole mystery of commodities', writes Marx, 'all the magic and necromancy that surrounds the products of labour on the basis of commodity production, vanishes [...] as soon as we come to other forms of production' (*ibid.*, 169). This is because historically, the majority of production in other societies involved making products for personal use. In contrast, commodities are made for exchange, and this opens up a new world of possibilities.

A close reading of the opening of *Capital* is immensely rewarding. The word 'appears' is there twice in the first paragraph, suggesting that Marx is acutely aware of the distinction between what something is, and how it looks. Marx is borrowing from Hegel's idea of essence and appearance, in the *Science of Logic* (1812). This distinction reminds us that things are often grasped not for what they are, but for how they appear to be. Already then, – in the first few sentences! – Marx is beginning to uncover the reality behind the appearance.

Wealth, in capitalist societies, 'appears' to be a collection of commodities. That wealth is synonymous with consumer products is, for Marx, the problem. For John Holloway, the first sentence is really about wealth, not the commodity (Holloway, 2015, 3). The original term Marx uses, '*Reichtum*', could have been translated as richness, which has a 'broader meaning: a rich tapestry, an enriching conversation, a rich life or experience, a rich diversity of colours' (*ibid.*, 3). For Holloway, Marx is asking: what would richness look like in a society beyond capitalism? Marx answers this question in an earlier work, the *Grundrisse der Kritik der Politischen Ökonomie* (*Foundations of a Critique of Political Economy*): wealth is 'the universality of individual needs, capacities, pleasures, productive forces etc. [...] the development of all human powers as such the end in itself, not as measured on a *predetermined yardstick*' (Marx, 1993, 488). For Marx, capitalist society recognises wealth only as a vast collection of commodities, not as human freedom, richness, potential, or ability.

The commodity, then, frustrates our efforts to attain freedom. The creation of commodities takes up most of our time (whether we work in a café, factory, or bookshop). So why do we have commodities? The commodity, writes Marx, is 'an external object, a thing which through its qualities satisfies human needs of whatever kind' (Marx, 1990, 125). This is what Marx calls its 'use-value', and this usefulness is 'conditioned by the physical properties of the commodity' (*ibid.*, 126). But the commodity has another value: it can be exchanged for something else and therefore has an exchange value. As swapping shoes for smartphones would be too tiresome and difficult, an independent form of value is needed. Marx defines money as the universal equivalent. Whether money is gold or silver; paper, as in the example at the start of this chapter; virtual (as numbers on a banking app); or even cryptocurrency like Bitcoin, makes no difference. Marx is not yet interested in the form that money takes, but in what it achieves: it allows the means of relating 'the values of two commodities' (*ibid.*, 139). Money allows the value of individual commodities to be expressed as price in capitalist markets. Money, as Marx makes clear, is only one part of the study of capital (he titles Part One of *Capital* 'Commodities and money', and has a chapter on money in the *Grundrisse*). Money, then, is a means to an end: it makes relationships possible. But in this act of exchange, in coming to buy a commodity, something strange begins to happen. To grasp the 'mystical character of the commodity' we must locate a suitable analogy. For Marx, 'we must take flight into the misty realm of religion', for only here can we see how the 'products of the human brain appear as autonomous figures endowed with a life of their own' (*ibid.*, 165). Marx wants to show how the modern-day worship of the commodity is a kind of religious inversion.

THE FETISHISM OF THE COMMODITY AND ITS SECRET

Part Four of the first chapter of *Capital* is the most frequently read in English studies. It contains Marx's idea of commodity fetishism, which is the best known of Marx's key ideas about capitalist economy. For Marx, a commodity is, at first sight 'an extremely obvious, trivial thing' (Marx, 1990, 163). As a use-value 'there is nothing mysterious about it' (*ibid.*, 163). It is perfectly clear that it has been created for a purpose. Marx gives an example: a wooden table. The wood has been altered to make the table, but the table is still wood, 'an ordinary sensuous thing'. But as a commodity, it changes, almost as if by magic. It 'stands on its head and evolves [...] grotesque ideas, far more wonderful than if it were to begin dancing of its own free will' (*ibid.*, 164). The commodity, then, appears increasingly magical, endowed with a will of its own. Its mystical power, 'clearly [...] arises from [its] form', but not its physical form. It comes from what Marx said was 'the form, which stamps value as exchange-value' (*ibid.*, 131). In using the literary fantastic (investing the commodity with supernatural powers), Marx gives voice to the uncanny experience of capitalism. Crucially, for Marx, when we look closely at the act of exchange, the operations of capitalist society are both real and fantastical.

It is the analysis of the commodity that brings out 'that it is a very strange thing' (*ibid.*, 163). Marx called commodities 'social hieroglyphs' which we must decipher to understand fully (*ibid.*, 167). For Marx, the commodity has a fetish, but this is a very different kind of thing to our common understanding of the term. Two points need to be clarified here. First, in capitalist cultures fetishism tends to refer to some strange attachment, fixation, or desire, often sexual in nature. This means that a 'broadly Freudian, psycho-sexual conception of fetishism has thus come to prevail, in the culture of capitalism, with which Marx's notion of commodity fetishism is often confused' (Osborne, 2006, 11). Second, Marx is not concerned with the psychological aspects of the commodity, such as the ways in which consumers can invest commodities with specific desires or wishes ('if only I had that pair of new shoes!').

Marx does not discuss consumer fetishism, but his analysis opens the door to it. What we call 'commodity aesthetics' is immensely important in cultural studies, and it examines the circulation of commodities in relation to advertising, design, and display (*ibid.*, 12). The most sustained cultural examination of the commodity form is the TV series *Mad Men* (2007–2015). Set in a fictional advertising agency on Madison Avenue in Manhattan, *Mad Men* offers a unique sociology, or social psychology, of commodities, in which creative directors and copywriters dream up ways to sell products. Advertising is an art, and a product is more likely to sell if a strong emotional bond can be created with the potential buyer. *Mad Men* goes further. 'Happiness' says Don Draper, 'is the smell of a new car' (*Mad Men*, Season 1, 2007). Draper is the most talented creative director at the agency. For him, inhaling the smell of a newly bought car is to experience happiness. But while *Mad Men* examines, in detail, the complexities of the commodity form, it also, at the same time, participates in promoting the 'immense collection of commodities' that Marx critiqued in the opening line of *Capital*.

Marx is outlining the fetish *character* of the commodity. For Marx, fetishism refers to the obfuscatory relations of capital, to the ways in which it is a system skilled in hiding its secrets. The term fetish refers to the talismanic qualities of the commodity, those objects that are believed to have an occult power over us. In attributing this power to commodities, Marx shows that capitalism sustains the belief that commodities have the power to make us, rather than us making them. For instance, I may buy Roger Federer's tennis racket because of the belief that it will make me a better tennis player. The racket, rather than the person, is perceived to be the origin of better play. The object – the tennis racket – seems to lend its power to us, rather than us to it. This investment of the commodity with supernatural powers is only possible, argues Marx, because we do not recognise this power as objectified *human* labour. Marx suggests that capitalism is a world of living commodities, rather than free humans.

This is because in capitalist production, objects become commodities through a division of labour, in which individuals 'do not come into social contact until they exchange the products of labour' (Marx, 1990, 165). The sphere of exchange mediates society. It is only through the commodity that we see the result of human labour (when you turn on a tap and water is released, you do not see all the labour involved, you only see the commodity: water). This character trait – obscuring the real relations of capitalism – is not a physical, objective, material part of the commodity, but a 'definite social relation' which assumes 'the fantastic form of a relation between things'. This fetish emerges 'from the peculiar social character of the labour which produces them' (*ibid.*, 165). In this world, 'the mysterious character of the commodity-form consists in the fact that the commodity represents the social characteristics of men's own labour as objective characteristics of the products of labour themselves, as the socio-natural properties of these things' (*ibid.*, 164–5).

THE WORKING DAY

Chapter Ten of *Capital* is where Marx talks about the physical bounds of the working day. A certain amount of value production from the labour process goes into paying wages, while the rest creates surplus value for the capitalist. Surplus value, as I mentioned at the beginning of the chapter, is the amount raised through the sale of the product minus the costs involved to make it. Capitalists want to generate as much surplus value as possible, and so are interested in a long working day. But it is impossible for workers to work the full 24 hours of a day. They would be mentally and physically exhausted. Workers, on the other hand, want the best possible pay for their labour, and want to spend part of their day in rest, relaxation, education, intellectual development, necessary social functions, hobbies, and so on. As such, there is a tension between the demands of workers and capitalists that must be sorted out, which is 'a struggle over the limits of [the working day], a struggle between collective capital i.e. the class of capitalists, and collective labour, i.e. the working class' (Marx, 1990, 344).

For Marx, this social relation – the capitalist buying the labour power of the worker – is exploitative. In entering into this arrangement, all humanity is lost, for as 'a capitalist, he is only capital personified. His soul is the soul of capital' (*ibid.*, 342). The capitalist becomes possessed of a demonic spirit and has only one aim in mind. Capital has only 'one sole driving force, the drive to valorize itself, to create surplus-value' to 'absorb the greatest possible amount of surplus labour' (*ibid.*, 342).

Marx turns to the gothic to make this clear. In a famous pronouncement on the monstrous nature of capital, he writes that

'Capital is dead labour which, vampire-like, lives only by sucking living labour, and lives the more, the more it sucks' (*ibid.*, 342). The time 'during which the worker works is the time during which the capitalist consumes the labour power he has brought from him' (*ibid.*, 342). The prolongation of the working day into the night 'only slightly quenches the vampire thirst for the living blood of labour'; the 'vampire will not let go while there remains a single muscle, sinew or drop of blood to be exploited' (*ibid.*, 367). Until humans can assert themselves as the subject of history, rather than its objects, this enslavement will continue. As Marx writes in the *Grundrisse*, the 'shortening of the working-day is its basic prerequisite' (Marx, 1993, 958–9). Using gothic imagery, Marx is able to show the true horror of the capitalist class, who appear as vampires sucking the life out of the working class. This is more than rhetorical flourish or extended textual licence. Capitalism, Marx suggests, turns living humans into lifeless creatures. One might say that *Capital* is a political economy of the dead (Neocleous, 2003, 668).

The American writer Herman Melville (1819–1891) addressed the relationship between workers and capitalists in his short story 'Bartleby the Scrivener: A Story of Wall Street' (1853). While not immediately recognisable as a gothic tale, the narrative contains death, vampirism, (mal)nourishment, and inhumanity. The narrator is an elderly Manhattan lawyer who hires a young clerk – a scrivener – Bartleby, to make copies of legal documents. At first, Bartleby produces a large amount of high-quality work, then, one day, decides he will do no more copying, preferring to spend long periods sleeping or staring out of the window. Bartleby is described as thin, pale, and exhausted, subsisting on a diet of ginger nuts. He barely utters a word, lacks any kind of life force, and seems depressed.

Bartleby fits all of the characteristics that Marx describes in his chapter on the working day. We see all of the gothic *effects* on Bartleby without being given any of the economic explanations. Copying out long law documents is a 'dull, wearisome, and lethargic affair' (Melville, 2009, 11). As the narrator remarks, 'I can readily imagine that to some sanguine temperaments it would be altogether intolerable. For example, I cannot credit that the mettlesome poet Byron would have contentedly sat down with Bartleby to examine a law document of, say five hundred pages, closely written in a crimpy hand (*ibid.*, 2009, 11). The invocation of the poet Byron (1788–1824) is crucial, signalling that there is no creativity, originality, or pleasure in Bartleby's work. This is why Bartleby has 'decided upon doing no more writing' (*ibid.*, 2009).

One of the most important aspects of Marx's chapter on the working day is the appearance of the 'voice of the worker, which had previously been stifled in the sound and the fury of the production process' (Marx, 1990, 342). Again, Marx acknowledges that the owner of the factory may be a good person, 'a model citizen, perhaps a member of the R.S.P.C.A.', but when they become a capitalist all ethical obligations are put to one side: 'the thing you represent when you come face to face with me has no heart in its breast' (*ibid.*, 343). The unnamed worker is given a voice, and makes a speech, demanding 'a normal working day because, like every other seller, I demand the value of my commodity', which is labour (*ibid.*, 343).

Bartelby does not give speeches, but pursues a course of quiet resistance. Crucially, he does not refuse to work, but advocates a preference, repeating throughout the story that 'he would prefer not to' (Melville, 2009, 13). Bartleby withdraws his labour from the lawyer. For Marxist critics, Bartleby is an embodiment of the alienated worker, copying out boring legal documents that have no relevance to his life. His function is to generate surplus value and protect the private property of the lawyer. His death, in the closing pages of the story, is the result of a detached, unethical, and amoral capitalist economy that does not recognise Bartleby as anything other than a worker. If Bartleby will not work, then nothing can be done for him. Both Marx and Melville – through theory and fiction – respond to the exploitative conditions of contemporary capitalism. They reveal how workers need to be seen as individual human beings, the subjects of their own lives. Marx advocated shortening the working day, which used to be 14 hours, six days a week. It was his youngest daughter, Eleanor Marx (1855–1898), a member of the trade union movement in England, who would help secure the eight-hour working day.

UNCOVERING THE SECRET

As I argued in the 'Why Marx?' section, *Capital* is a text rich in secrets, symbols, riddles, and allusions. Like a modernist novel, it contains hundreds of characters, open-ended symbols, and the juxtaposition of voices and events. In the final section, I will pay close attention to *Capital* as a narrative, as a rich multi-layered masterpiece.

For students of English, the most important part of *Capital* is narrative structure. Marx uses a dialectical structure that regards everything as 'being in a fluid state, in motion' (Marx, 1990, 103). As I argued in Chapter Two, Marx uses dialectics as a mode of argument to reveal the movement of capitalism. Being able to see the movement of capital was crucial to understanding it. Marx wrote eloquently on the many ways in which capital attempts to hide the realities of exploitation and oppression through procedures of mystification and obfuscation. At the close of Part Two of *Capital*, Marx invites us:

> in company with the owner of money and the owner of labour-power [to] leave this noisy sphere, where everything takes place on the surface and in full-view of everyone, and follow them into the hidden abode of production, on whose threshold hangs the notice 'No admittance except on business'.
>
> (Marx, 1990, 279–280)

Promising to unveil its secrets, 'we shall see, not only how capital produces, but how capital is itself produced. The secret of profit-making must be laid bare' (*ibid.*, 280).

For Marx, 'a scientific analysis of competition is possible only if we can grasp the inner nature of capital, just as the apparent motions of the heavenly bodies are intelligible only to someone who is acquainted with their real motions, which are not perceptible to the senses' (*ibid.*, 433). Movement is socially necessary for capital to function effectively. For Marx, capital is restless, ever in flux, and seeking endless accumulation. Ultimately, this means that:

> any pause or even a slowdown in that motion for whatever reason means a loss of value, which may be resuscitated in part or *in toto* only when the

> motion of capital is resumed. When capital takes on a particular form – as a production process, as a product waiting to be sold, as a commodity circulating in the hands of merchant capitalists, as money waiting to be transferred or reinvested – then capital is 'virtually devalued'. Capital lying 'at rest' in any of these states is variously termed 'negated', 'fallow', 'dormant' or 'fixated'.
>
> (Harvey, 2017, 74)

Capital must move. It can only be realised as capital if it circulates. But what kind of movement does capital enact? As Marx makes clear, there is a real difference between external movement (how capital appears to move) and intrinsic movement (how it really moves). All these contradictions come out in Marx's analysis: capital is fixed but must move, it is attached but capable of detaching itself at any time. In *Capital*, Marx makes an effort to understand just how capital moves.

In *Capital*, Marx set out his aim to 'reveal the laws of motion of modern society', but he cannot do this through static or fixed categories. Here we come back to the representational dilemma sketched out at the beginning. The concepts that Marx uses must move; over the course of his critique, they must become richer, deeper, referring to each other as the book advances. Marx's method, like the economic relationships he explores, must contain movement, circulation, and change. Marx starts with surface appearances before moving to disclose deep concepts that can only be understand on the completion of his book. Rather than build an argument brick by brick, Marx starts with outward appearances, moves through layers of external reality to the conceptual core, then grows the argument outward again, returning to the surface through layers of theory (Harvey, 2017, 10). Marx's critique of the capitalist mode of production is undoubtedly his most impressive achievement, but the narrative structure that he develops is immensely rich. Marx never completed his proposed treaty on dialectical criticism, although he left behind, as Ernest Mandel reminds us, the 'striking application of [the] dialectical method' in *Capital* (Marx, 1990, 19). Over his life, Marx never produced any major theoretical expositions, so his methodologies must be reconstructed from his writings on economics, history, and politics.

THE *GRUNDRISSE*

A key text in helping us think about Marx's methodologies is the *Grundrisse*. Written between 1857 and 1858, this text was an important preparatory work to *Capital*. Marx returned to his economic studies with the arrival of the long-awaited financial crisis in 1857. Public panic began after a bank collapse in New York, which spread to Europe and reached England in October. Plummeting prices and bankruptcies did nothing for public confidence. There was increasingly widespread acknowledgment of the inevitability, and for radicals even the desirability, of crisis. Both Marx and Engels saw an opportunity for revolution; Engels was in jubilant spirits, writing that the 'general appearance of the [cotton] Exchange here was truly delightful' (Engels, *MECW40*, 106). Marx kept an eye on these events, collating material, writing notes, and producing a manuscript of 800 pages. The *Grundrisse* (translated as *Foundations*) is a series of seven roughly drafted notebooks written for the purposes of self-clarification. Like most of Marx's works, the *Grundrisse* is a 'text of transition [...] a frenetic, and genial, intellectual notetaking' (Bellofiore, 2013, 3). It casts a fresh light on the writing of *Capital*, meaning that a comparative exercise of these two texts reveals substantial rewards. But the notebooks were not published until the middle of the twentieth century, and were translated into English only in 1973.

Included in the *Grundrisse* is Marx's famous 'Fragment on Machines'. It is a central section for understanding a theory of capitalist crisis as a description of the process in which a new mode of production emerges, created by capitalism but also in contradiction with its basic logic (Heinrich, 2013, 197). It contains a critical section where technology dominates production and human labour is merely supervision. These comments are particularly important in a world where capitalism will increasingly rely on artificial intelligence and robotics.

MARX AND THE MACHINES

One of the major challenges for every society is dealing with the development of new technologies. In *The Poverty of Philosophy*

(1847), Marx illustrates this point with the help of a medieval example: 'The hand-mill gives you society with the feudal lord; the steam-mill society with the industrial capitalist' (Marx, *MECW6*, 165–66). Marx, however, was not a technological determinist, and the aphorism is likely a joke about all that is wrong with productive force determinism. There is much in his writings that cannot be captured by new inventions and innovative processes. But Marx did produce notebooks on technology and was aware that, as he wrote in *Capital*, 'Technology discloses man's mode of dealing with Nature, the process of production by which he sustains life, and thereby also lays bare the mode of formation of his social relations, and of the mental conceptions that flow from them' (Marx, 1990, 493). Technology, then, is crucial to understanding Marx's understanding of historical change and development.

The 'Fragment on Machines' is deep within the *Grundrisse*. It reveals that Marx recognises capitalism's tendency to replace human and animal labour with machines. Competition compels innovation, leading to changes in processes and technology. As capitalists are ever on the hunt for ways to increase surplus value and reduce necessary labour time, they substitute workers for machines. This is not freedom proper because it still entails suffering and exploitation. For Marx:

> Capital employs machinery, rather, only to the extent that it enables the worker to work a larger part of his time for capital, to relate to a larger part of his time as time which does not belong to him, to work longer for another. Through this process, the amount of labour necessary for the production of a given object is indeed reduced to a minimum, but only in order to realize a maximum of labour in the maximum number of such objects. The first aspect is important, because capital here – quite unintentionally – reduces human labour, expenditure of energy, to a minimum. This will redound to the benefit of emancipated labour, and is the condition of its emancipation.
> (Marx, 1993, 701)

Marx recognises the contradiction: machines reduce labour without creating collective wealth. Under a less rapacious system, machines represent an immense opportunity for human flourishing. Automation has the potential to change the relationship between labour and capital. Marx has already described other changes in technology 'merely as a formal modification', but automation enacts something much deeper:

> Once adopted into the production process of capital, the means of labour passes through different metamorphoses, whose culmination is the [...] automatic system of machinery [...] set in motion by an automaton, a moving power that moves itself; this automaton consisting of numerous mechanical and intellectual organs, so that the workers themselves are cast merely as its conscious linkages.
>
> (Marx, 1993, 692)

Under this new process, the activity of the worker also changes. This is 'not a matter of chance for capital, but the historical transformation of the traditional means of labour, as handed down from the past' (*ibid.*, 693). Now, Marx writes, 'the accumulation of knowledge and skill, of the general productive forces of the social mind, is thus absorbed in capital as opposed to labour, and hence appears as a property of capital' (*ibid.*). In the nineteenth century, machinery had an increasing significance in capitalist production, and the individual worker played a smaller role in the sense of the contribution of his knowledge and skill, as in forms of artisanal production. With the development of new technological processes, resulting in a diminished space for labour, what then does the worker contribute? Marx writes that 'Labour no longer appears so much as included in the production process, but rather man relates himself to that process as overseer and regulator [...] he stands beside the production process, rather than being its main agent' (*ibid.*, 705).

Workers no longer provide immediate labour in sense of crafting a table, 'it is the machine which possesses skill and strength in place of the worker, is itself the virtuoso, with a soul of its own in the mechanical laws acting through it; and it consumes coal or oil just as the worker consumes food to keep up its perpetual motion' (*ibid.*, 693). Here Marx makes a profound contribution while raising philosophical questions about the future of work, machines, and robotics, which we are only beginning to examine.

MARX AND THE *NEW-YORK TRIBUNE*

Capital took some 18 years to write, meaning that Marx was preoccupied with other tasks and activities. He returned to journalism, but only out of financial necessity. In 1848, when in Cologne, Marx had met the young American editor Charles A. Dana of the *New-York Tribune*. Marx became a foreign correspondent, writing on the opium trade, revolution, factory labour, starvation, and Ireland. He would later boast that the toil involved in writing these articles to pay the rent amounted to crushing up and grinding bones to make a soup for the paupers in the workhouse (Marx, 2010, xx). But journalism afforded Marx an audience and an outlet for his views.

Marx's letters on India are particularly interesting. The British took control of the continent in 1858, after a rebellion the year before. The violence of the British forces had led Marx to write several impassioned attacks on torture and collective punishment. While the British East India Company seized control of Indian markets, capitalism was transforming the subcontinent through the introduction of steamships, communications, and railways. In an 1853 letter to the *New-York Tribune*, Marx denounced the violence of British colonial rule and offered a critique of the problems of pre-capitalist India. England 'was actuated only by the vilest interests' in acquiring India, and 'was stupid in her manner of enforcing' social and political change – but, Marx proposed, 'whatever […] the crimes of England she was the unconscious tool of history in bringing about that revolution' (Marx, 2010, 306). Horrified by the brutality of European conquest, Marx saw no use in overthrowing foreign domination simply to restore the previous system. As Marx writes,

> sickening as it must be to human feeling to witness those myriads of industrious patriarchal and inoffensive social organizations disorganized and dissolved into their units, thrown into a sea of woes, and their individual members losing at the same time their ancient form of civilization, and their hereditary means of subsistence, we must not forget that these idyllic village-communities, inoffensive though they may appear, had always been the solid foundation of Oriental despotism.

> (Marx, 2010, 306)

Imperialism was a detestable practice, but it would create new networks of global capitalist exchange.

Marx made numerous financial appeals to the *New-York Tribune*, but they were all refused. The family was increasingly impoverished, and most of their belongings were in and out of pawnshops. The situation of the family was captured by a Prussian spy, writing in 1852 that

> Marx lives in one of the worst – therefore, one of the cheapest – quarters of London. He occupies two rooms [...] Everything is broken down, tattered and torn, with a half inch of dust over everything [...] A seller of second-hand good would be ashamed to give away such a remarkable collection of odds and ends.
>
> (McLellan, 1973, 35)

The report captures the existence of the family, torn between middle-class connections and penury. Marx learned about the workings of capitalism from his intensive reading in the British Museum, but he learned about the domestic situation of the working class first-hand: 'it was a life lived in crowded rooms [...] a life in debt to bakers and grocers and butchers; a life in which a purchase often had to be balanced out by selling or pawning some previous purchase' (Stallybrass, 1998, 191). As a working-class family, the 'hopes and despairs of the Marxes could be traced by their [frequent] journeys to the pawnbrokers' (*ibid.*).

SUMMARY

Capital was Marx's masterwork. In it, he set out to discover the laws of motion that govern the movement of the capitalist mode of production. In this chapter, I explored Marx's powerful analysis of capital, the commodity (fetishism of the commodity), and the working day. I also discussed how Marx presents his ideas through a dialectical structure. An important companion text to *Capital* is the *Grundrisse*. This text was originally the first draft of *Capital*, and was written around the time of the financial panic that occurred in 1857. It contains Marx's ideas on machines, technology, money, capital, and automation. The *Grundrisse*, however, was not published until 1939. We are only starting to scratch the surface of this astonishing text.

5

LITERATURE AND CAPITALISM

In Sally Rooney's novel *Normal People*, Connell and Marianne wander around an empty housing estate near their school. Nicknamed 'the ghost' because nobody lives there, the teenagers speculate on why the houses are 'lying empty' (Rooney, 2018, 34). As Connell asks, 'Why don't they give them away if they can't sell them? I'm not being thick with you, I'm genuinely asking' (*ibid.*, 34). Both recognise that there is something wrong with the empty houses but neither understands why. 'It's something to do with capitalism', Marianne says. 'That's the problem', Connell replies, 'Everything is' (*ibid.*, 34). Here, the two teenagers understand something important about capitalism. Houses have been built but, because they cannot be sold, they are left empty. From the standpoint of satisfying immediate human needs, this is completely irrational. If there is a quantity of empty houses, and there are people who require somewhere to live, the solution seems obvious. However, within a system built on profit and the extraction of surplus value, having empty houses is perfectly rational. In this example, Rooney's novel details some of the ways in which capitalism is a contradictory system, prompting readers to reflect on the difficulties of home ownership.

Incidentally, Rooney has described herself as a Marxist. In an interview, she gives an articulate reading of her novel in relation to the social and economic pressures of global capitalism. 'In my own life', Rooney says, 'the way that I think about the world that we live in is [...] mostly through a sort of Marxist framework' (Rooney, 2019). Given this admission, coupled with the critical aspects of the narrative sketched above, I would suggest that *Normal People* is a novel that reflects on capitalist ideologies through the prism of more politically progressive modes.

As the most influential analysis of capitalism, Marx's work is immensely useful for understanding literature. As I argued in Chapter Four, Marx's *Capital* is a literary work, but he also used literature to shape his key ideas. The works of William Shakespeare (1564–1616), Honoré de Balzac (1799–1850), and Charles Dickens (1812–1870) gave Marx a way of understanding social relationships within and beyond capitalism. Marx thought that while 'many authors are spokesmen for a dominant class, great literature is able to rise above a prevalent ideology. When this happens, it may constitute [...] a realm in which an author can express himself – to a considerable extent – as a total human being' (Prawer, 2011, 404). Marx's use of texts shows literature was at the heart of his critical vision.

MARX'S LITERARY CRITICISM

For Marx, Shakespeare was a writer who understood money. In *Timon of Athens* (1607), money is a commodity that distorts human relationships. The central character, Timon, gives away money wastefully, with everyone seeking to please him in order to get more. When Timon loses his money, these friendships turn out to be hollow. Destitute, Timon refers to money as a 'yellow slave' and the 'common whore of mankind' (Shakespeare, 2007, 1781). Shakespeare shows money to be a destructive commodity that corrodes human relationships. For Marx, writing in the *Economic and Philosophical Manuscripts*, Shakespeare brings out 'two properties of money in particular: firstly, money transforms all human and natural qualities into their opposites, the universal confusion and inversion of things' (Marx, 1992, 377). In the play, Timon's friends are false friends; they simply wish to be given money. Secondly, money is the 'universal whore, the universal pimp of men and peoples' (*ibid.*). For Marx, the whole business of money is synonymous with prostitution and misanthropic acts.

Marx's comments are more than mere explications of the play. His sympathetic reading of Shakespeare captures the disillusioned idealism of modern society, where all relationships belong to the world of the cash-nexus. Such criticisms are central to Marx's views on capitalism. They show that literature was central: that 'Shakespeare was one of the spiritual godfathers of the *Communist Manifesto* [...] Marx would doubtless have become a communist even if he had never read *Timon of Athens*, but his reading of that play helped him to crystalize his ideas' (Muir, 1993, 99).

Marx gives a more detailed literary criticism in an exchange of letters over a historical drama by Ferdinand Lassalle (1825–1864). The play is about a German knight, *Franz von Sickingen* (1858). Marx begins with 'the formal aspects first' stressing that the long speeches make the play almost impossible to perform on stage (*MECW40*, 440). The 'chief protagonists [...] *are* representative of certain classes and tendencies, hence of certain ideas of their time, and derive their motives not from the petty appetites of the individual but from the very historical current by which they are borne along' (*ibid.*, 440). But the weakness of the play was that the 'peasant movement deserved closer attention' (*ibid.*, 440). Lassalle had failed to account for the experience of the peasant class and its relation to other classes. Marx is arguing that understanding class categories is a crucial arena for a correct historical understanding. Fredric Jameson explains that the real cause of the knight's downfall in the play is not his tragic flaw, but 'a social' flaw:

> Sickingen could never have had the support of the revolutionary peasants because his basic social aim was utterly different from theirs, focused not on a liberation of the land but on reestablishment of the petty nobility, which itself suffered from the domination of the great princes and of the church. Thus, for Marx and Engels the tragic situation of Sickingen was an objective one and had nothing to do with any agonizing moral choices inside his mind, any grandiloquent moral postures he might strike on stage.
>
> (Jameson, 1971, 192–93)

The issue is first economic and political – that is, material – and not moral or rhetorical. For Marx, *Franz von Sickingen* was a historical play not sufficiently true to history. As Marx developed his ideas about the historical role of the working class and the role of political and economic forces in human development, he would come to stress the situated, contextual character of human beings.

In pointing out the formal weaknesses, such as the endless speeches and the stress on forces that were not decisive, Marx did not feel that all characters should be read as symbols for specific types. There is the potential here for a vulgar 'Marxist' criticism that would reduce all figures into obvious allegories or reflections of real people. But Marx's criticism is deeply attentive to the logic of the text itself, and draws out specific failures in the narrative that reveal an understanding of literary form. Marx's reading acts as an introduction to the application to literature of his social and economic ideas, which would later become Marxist literary criticism. But crucially, Marx and Engels were hesitant in using literature for political revolution. Politics comes second to the requirements of formal ingenuity, composition, and expression. For both, literary works were valuable aesthetic endeavours in their own right, and not simply tools for communist revolution.

MARXIST LITERARY CRITICISM

Marx and Engels never produced a systematic theory of art, literature, or culture. Some Marxists suggest there could be a uniform approach to interpreting texts, while others argue that, because Marxist critique stresses critical responses to political and historical moments, no single theory could work. For instance, Imre Szeman argues there is no *singular* set of considerations, aims, or objectives that define Marxist literary criticism (Szeman, 2009, 38). This may appear disappointing to those of you approaching Marxist criticism for the first time; on reflection, however, it would certainly be troubling if we did have one unitary approach because it would mean we are unable to invent new and fresh ways of reading Marx, and that we are unable to move beyond traditional readings of literary texts.

There is a persistent, but mistaken, assumption guiding the writing of many textbooks over the past several decades in which criticism comprises a set of approaches corresponding to specific perspectives and disciplines (Foley, 2019, 87). Students are often encouraged to select and apply one of a variety of critical paradigms, such as new criticism, psychoanalysis, feminism, queer theory, race studies, postcolonialism, post-structuralism, eco-criticism, affect theory, historicism, or Marxism. Such a methodological assumption is frequently accompanied by the idea that these approaches are best deployed in connection with texts whose explicit subject matter clearly relates to the chosen perspective or discipline. For instance, nineteenth-century novels seemingly committed to revolutionary social transformation naturally align with Marxism; while poems on melting polar ice caps are best assigned to eco-critical modes of enquiry. For Foley, this approach is especially constraining when applied to Marxist literary criticism: 'often held to be relevant only to texts produced during the capitalist era and directly reflecting economic relationships and class conflicts' (*ibid.*, 88).

As we have seen so far, Marx's work reveals a critical and rigorous conceptual knowledge that exists beyond such general or typical features. Marxism seeks to enrich our understanding of literary texts by moving beyond personal and private registers to read a text in relation to a specific historical moment or situation. Done correctly, this results in an expansion of the meaning of literary texts, an enlargement of their critical resonance, and an increase of their complexity. In Chapter Six, I will look at some major Marxist critics who take these ideas forward.

SUMMARY

Literature was central to the development of Marx's political vision. His reading of Shakespeare's *Timon of Athens* was particularly important in his account of money, in the *Economic and Philosophical Manuscripts*. In reading Shakespeare closely, Marx saw that money is a destructive commodity that corrodes human relationships. In his literary criticism of the texts of his own time, it is clear that Marx did not establish formulas by which literary works should be read. Instead, Marx's criticism proposes interpretative resources and possibilities, prompting us to reflect on issues of class, history, and form.

6

BASE AND SUPERSTRUCTURE

When we read best-selling books, go to the cinema, drink a beer, visit a museum, or see an advertisement, we tend to ignore the political economy that hammers culture into shape. For the most part, none of these activities appears to have a discernible political component. But behind each is a complex network of decisions and drives that need to be understood in relation to the contradictions and crisis-tendencies of capitalism.

As I argued in Chapter One, Marx first turned to political economy while living in Paris and writing the *Economic and Philosophical Manuscripts*. He criticised the work of political economists for defending private property, because he saw this as an exploitative arrangement where the property owner takes possession of the wealth created by the worker. For Marx, this exploitation is at the centre of capitalist society. The whole point of Marx's immersion in political economy, however, was to arrive at a point beyond it. He even wrote to Engels of his occasional boredom with 'the whole economic shit' (Marx, *MECW38*, 325), but it was only through an immersive study of political economy that Marx believed he could arrive at truly original insights. Marx rejected capitalist ownership of production, took seriously the hardships of individual workers, and proposed a radical democratic communist politics.

In this chapter, I will do three things. First, I will examine in detail one of Marx's most important ideas: the connection between culture and economics – the base and superstructure. Second, I will discuss how later Marxist thinkers – notably Louis Althusser (1918–1990), Fredric Jameson (1934–), and Raymond Williams (1921–1988) – have developed Marx's ideas for thinking seriously about literature and culture. Third, I will use a short story, 'The Necklace' (1884) by the French writer Guy de Maupassant (1850–1893), as an example to show how Marx's ideas can be used to produce a Marxist literary criticism.

It is worth stating at the outset that base and superstructure remain one of the most contested aspects of Marx's critical thought. There are numerous readings that have oversimplified this argument, contending that Marx believes economic forces to determine everything about the way we live in the world, from the kind of coffee we drink to the music we enjoy. To think that Marx is reducing all forms of social life to an expression of merely economic interests is a kind of vulgar or mechanical Marxism: a poor, weak, or even lazy reading that substitutes critical nuance by cut-and-dried schematisations. It is crucial to see that the base and superstructure is not a blueprint, but a provisional sketch, a conceptual starting point. It is an incomplete intervention. In the following section I will explain the base and superstructure, paying special attention to its distinctive features, technical astuteness, and theoretical richness.

BASICS OF THE BASE AND SUPERSTRUCTURE

Let's begin with the key elements: What is the base? What is the superstructure? And where does Marx explore these ideas? Marx divides societies into their economic base (sometimes called the infrastructure) and cultural superstructure (the political, legal, and ideological forms that develop out of the base). As a diagram, this is often represented as two tiers (with the base as the bottom and the superstructure above) – although, as we will see, this has been challenged by later Marxist critics such as Louis Althusser (1918–1990). But the base and superstructure is more than a mechanical correspondence between economics and culture: it is a carefully constructed calibration.

There are three other important points here. First, the base is the sum total of productive economic relationships, not individual elements such as the working class. Second, the superstructure develops unevenly in different societies, accounting for cultural, political, and ideological difference. Even in a globalised world, culture develops differently in different nations. Zia Haider Rahman's novel *In the Light of What We Know* (2014) perfectly captures the uneven flow of finance capital around the world, moving from Wall Street to Sylhet in Bangladesh, from Kabul to London to Islamabad, from the United States to Afghanistan, showing how decisions made in boardrooms and on trading floors in London and New York have repercussions around the world. Rahman's novel shows the condition of modern global capitalism, but it also reveals complex cultural differences, particularly in the ways in which nations are differently gripped by global forces. As such, when considering Marx's idea of the base and superstructure, we need to think about moving from the local to the global. Third, base and superstructure are reciprocal: the base determines the superstructure 'only in the last instance'. Engels defended this idea in a letter of 1890:

According to the materialist conception of history, the *ultimately* determining element in history is the production and reproduction of real life. Other than this neither Marx nor I have ever asserted. Hence if somebody twists this into saying that the economic element is the *only* determining one, he transforms that proposition into a meaningless, abstract, senseless phrase. The economic situation is the basis, but the various elements of the superstructure – political forms of the class struggle and its results, to wit: constitutions established by the victorious class after a successful battle, etc., juridical forms, and even the reflexes of all these actual struggles in the brains of the participants, political, juristic, philosophical theories, religious views and their further development into systems of dogmas – also exercise their influence upon the course of the historical struggles and in many cases preponderate in determining their *form*.

(Engels, *MECW49*, 34–35)

As Engels argued, it is only after the complex interaction of elements that 'the economic movement finally asserts itself as necessary' (*ibid.*). In doing so, he wished to indicate that the economic – definitive in the final analysis – is itself subject to interaction with the superstructure. The economic is the base, but the factors of the superstructure – class struggle, legal structures, religion, and philosophy – all have a bearing on history. 'We make our history ourselves', writes Engels, echoing Marx, but under 'definite premises and conditions. Of these, the economic are ultimately decisive. But the political, etc., and even the traditions still lingering in people's minds, play some, if not a decisive, role.' (*ibid.*, 35). Engels offers an important concession. 'If some younger writers attribute more importance to the economic aspect than is its due,' he argues, 'Marx and I are to some extent to blame. We had to stress this leading principle in the face of opponents who denied it, and we did not always have the time, space, or opportunity to do justice to the other factors' (*ibid.*, 36). For Marx and Engels, culture is not reducible to economics, but economic factors are central to its development.

Marx did not suddenly arrive at the idea of the base and superstructure. It is a product of his long and intense study of politics and economics. Traces of the base and superstructure idea can be detected in his earlier works. In an important passage from *The German Ideology*, Marx and Engels present a reading of historical development which has become known, in the words of Engels, as the materialist conception of history:

> The production of ideas, of conceptions, of consciousness, is at first directly interwoven with the material activity and material intercourse of man – the language of real life. Conceiving, thinking, the mental intercourse of man at this stage still appear as the direct efflux of their material behaviour [...] we do not set out from what men say, imagine, conceive, nor from men as narrated, thought of, imagined, conceived, in order to arrive at men in the flesh. We set out from real, active men [...] Life is not determined by consciousness, but consciousness by life.
>
> (Marx, *MECW5*, 36–37)

In the same text, Marx writes about 'the social organisation evolving directly out of production and commerce, which in all ages forms the basis of the state and the rest of the idealistic superstructure' (ibid, 57). That fact that Marx underlines the effectivity of the idea demonstrates its importance within his work.

In other words, the starting point for understanding human existence is not a series of ideas, about God, the good life, or indeed anything else. People may change their ideas about the world, but real change can come about only by changing real social and economic relations, their relationship to nature and the natural world, and institutional structures. For Marx, it is the forces and relations of production that shape the lives of men and women. This means rejecting non-tangible realities for the fundamental components of human existence. For Marx, comprehending reality means first pushing through false doctrines to see the dynamics of material existence.

PREFACE TO *A CONTRIBUTION TO THE CRITIQUE OF POLITICAL ECONOMY*

Marx proposes base and superstructure in the preface to *A Contribution to the Critique of Political Economy* (1859). The full work is not particularly interesting as the ideas it expounds are more fully developed in *Capital*, which I examined in Chapter Four. Students reading Marx for the first time are often provided with this preface. Rich in its brevity, ir is perfect for a lively seminar discussion. It contains the first detailed account of the materialist conception of history (Marx had briefly mentioned this in *The German Ideology*), and his division of human societies into two main areas: economic realities – by which Marx means the ways in which people produce the essentials of life, such as the use of tools, machines factories, raw materials, and all the classes who participate in this activity, including the capitalist and the worker; and culture in the very broadest sense – including politics, religion, ideology, literature, and the family.

Marx begins the preface to *A Contribution to the Critique of Political Economy* with a short intellectual autobiography. In the full book he follows a linear structure, examining '*capital, landed property, wage-labour; the State, foreign trade, world market*' (Marx, 1992, 424, italics in original). He is setting out a detailed contents list. The chapter on capital, for instance, contains sections on the commodity, the circulation of capital, and capital in general, all of which he fully explores in his bigger work, *Capital*. All these sections have all been written separately and Marx has combined them in the finished work. But even as just a contents list, this gives us a clue to Marx's thought. To focus on one aspect of capital is not enough; Marx sees everything as connected, and he wants to give a complete picture of capitalism in all its complexity. Any one of these areas (capital, property, wage-labour, the state, foreign trade, the world market) would be a lifetime's study, but for Marx it is only by confronting them all that we can fully understand the complexities of capitalism.

For Marx, this all came about when he was editor at the *Rheinische Zeitung*. As I discussed in Chapter One, the 'theft' of wood caused Marx to turn his 'attention to economic questions' (*ibid.*, 424). Remember, Marx moved from philosophical ideas to political and economic contexts, as he was concerned with the daily realities of people who were criminalised for using wood from the forest. The 'general conclusion' that Marx reached 'became the guiding principle' of his studies. For Marx, 'in the social production of their existence, men inevitably enter into definite relations, which are independent of their will, namely relations of production' (*ibid.*, 425). These 'material forces' – which include relations of production (the social relationships people must enter into in order to survive) and means of production (tools, machines, factories, land) – constitute the 'economic stricture of society, the real foundation, on which arises a legal and political superstructure' (*ibid.*). The central point Marx is making is that the 'mode of production of material life conditions the general process of social, political, and intellectual life' (*ibid.*). This means that it is not ideas that determine people's existence, as Hegel would have it, but social existence that determines ideas.

For Marx, then, the 'real foundation' is the economic structure, but this structure is neither simple nor straightforward. As I argued in Chapter Four, capitalism is a mode of production that is skilful and accomplished in hiding its secrets. For Marx, the forces and relations of production shape society by imposing limits to the superstructure. This means that political and ideological relations can still develop relatively independently, and in turn changes at this level affect the course of economic development. But for Marx, the economic base is only the starting point for understanding change in society.

CONSEQUENCES FOR LITERATURE

In the previous section, I argued that Marx constructs a careful reading of the relationship between economics and culture, suggesting that economic realities condition culture, ideas, and politics. The preface is an important document, and prompts questions about the relationship between economics and culture. Marxism has long grappled with these questions, attempting to discern, with varying levels of success, the extent to which the economic foundation of a society determines the intellectual forces operating within it.

The complexity of this problem has resulted in some bitter disputes. Fredric Jameson remarks that 'nowhere has the Marxian doctrine of base and superstructure been more damaging than in Marxism itself, where the specialists of the base – the commentators on capitalism, the strategists of revolution – are encouraged to feel little more than contempt for the culture workers of the superstructure' (Jameson, 2014, 4). But Marx and Engels routinely questioned the role of culture in economics, and argued for a historical interpretation. However, Marx's remarks on aesthetics are tentative, occasionally in conflict, and dependent on complex concepts such as ideology (Nelson and Grossberg, 1988, 2). As the Marxist art critic John Berger writes, the relationship between culture and economics is a:

> question which Marx posed but could not answer: If art in the last analysis is a superstructure of an economic base, why does its power to move us endure long after the base has been transformed? Why, asked Marx, do we still look towards Greek art as an ideal? He began to answer the question [...] and then broke off the manuscript and was far too occupied ever to return.
>
> (Berger, 2016, 47)

Berger is here discussing a famous passage in Marx's *Grundrisse*. In it, Marx reflects on the relation of Greek art to the present moment. Why is it, he asks, that Greek poetry can afford such lasting pleasure when made by undeveloped productive forces? Surely, this is part of its appeal. Myth is the material of Greek art, leading Marx to propose a series of rhetorical questions: 'is Achilles possible with powder and lead?' or 'the *Iliad* with the printing press' (Marx, 1993, 111). Marx is satisfied that it is impossible to recreate Greek art in the modern world, but for Marx 'the difficulty lies not in understanding that the Greek arts and epic are bound up with certain forms of social development. The difficulty is that they still afford us artistic pleasure' (*ibid*.). The challenge, then, was to accept the irrevocable loss of a world that had produced such art and to comprehend the nature of the changes that had brought this about:

> A man cannot become a child again, or he becomes childish. But does he not find joy in the child's naïvité, and must he himself not strive to reproduce its truth at a higher stage? Does not the true character of each epoch come alive in the nature of its children? Why should not the historic childhood of humanity, its most beautiful unfolding, as a stage never to return, exercise an eternal charm? There are unruly children and precocious children. Many of the old peoples belong in this category. The Greeks were normal children. The charm of their art for us is not in contradiction to the undeveloped stage of society on which it grew. [It] is its result, rather, and is inextricably bound up, rather, with the fact that the unripe social conditions under which it arose, and could alone arise, can never return.
>
> (Marx, 1993, 111)

This passage has often served hostile critics eager to position Marx's reading of past art as a nostalgic lapse into childhood. Read in context, however, Marx argues that Greek art is attractive not despite, but because of, the undeveloped state of Greek society. Such societies had not yet undergone the division of labour intrinsic to capitalist relations of production, the shift from quality to quantity, and the development of productive forces. Absolved of the demands of commodity production, the limitations of Greek society paradoxically produced aesthetic works of great charm and lasting beauty.

Marxist critics have provided many interpretations of the idea of base and superstructure. Althusser argues that the 'economic is never clearly visible' meaning 'it does not coincide with any "given" [...] reality' (ibid., 173). In Althusser:

> the more narrowly economic – the forces of production, the labour process, technical development, or relations of production, such as the functional interrelation of social classes – is, however privileged, not identical with the mode of production as a whole, which assigns this narrowly "economic" level its particular function and efficiency as it does all the others.
>
> (Jameson, 2002, 21)

Althusser argues against a simple 'economic' reality, and for a structural, complex causality in which the totality is a structure of effects without obvious causes. Jameson agrees with Althusser that the mode of production is not just to do with economics and labour: instead, the economic is only one aspect of a wider sense of the mode of production, which includes cultural aspects.

Another reading of base and superstructure is provided by the Welsh Marxist Raymond Williams. Williams likewise rejected the economic reductionism of Marxist theory, proposing that such strict readings had impoverished Marx's writings. In a characteristically considered approach, Williams dwells on 'determination', a word of 'great linguistic and theoretical complexity':

> Marx uses the word which becomes, in English translation, 'determines' [...] Nevertheless, the particular history and continuity of the term serves to remind us that there are, within ordinary use – and this is true of most of the major European languages – quite different possible meanings and implications of the word determine. There is, on the one hand, from its theological inheritance, the notion of an external cause which totally predicts or prefigures, indeed totally controls a subsequent activity. But there is also, from the experience of social practice, a notion of determination as setting limits, exerting pressures.
>
> (Williams, 1973, 120)

For Williams, the superstructure is never simply a reflex or reflection of the economic plane. Its determination by the base is always a question of limits and pressures, of complex interacting elements within a totality of social relations (*ibid.*, 6). Inherent in Williams' approach is the necessity to figure out the exact relationship of the base to superstructure as it fluctuates under changing historical conditions. Jameson pursues this further, arguing the base and superstructure is not really a model,

> but a starting point and a problem, something as undogmatic as an imperative simultaneously to grasp culture in and for itself, but also in relationship to its outside, its content, its context, and its space of intervention and of effectivity. How one does that, however, is never given in advance.
>
> (Jameson, 1989, 42)

Following the work of other Marxists, my approach in this book is to encourage you to see the base and superstructure as the sketching of a problem that Marx outlines, but does not solve. Marx does not offer a model or formula that can be applied in advance of history. His contribution is less a blueprint or solution to contemporary society than an invitation to reflect on how we can connect culture to economics. Marx's genius is to highlight the richness of this relationship. But Marxism must reflect new historical developments. It is a mode of thought especially attentive to the circumstances in which it operates, and so a deep knowledge of history is essential. For those of us interested in literature, Marx's idea of the base and superstructure immediately situates the text in dialogue with historical developments (literary, cultural, social, political, ideological, and economic), compelling us to move back and forth between text and world. This is the task of Marxist literary criticism. In the following section we will see how Marx's ideas can elucidate texts.

'THE NECKLACE'

In this section we will use 'The Necklace' (1884), a short story written by French writer Guy Maupassant (1850–1893), as a conceptual starting point to discuss how Marx's ideas can interpret literary texts. Actually, interpretation is the wrong word. For Marxists, literary texts are already interpretations of the world in which an individual author, often with other people (editors and publishers), reworks the raw material of language, ideas, and narrative history – a shared repertoire of conventions and practices – to create a particular work. Rather, texts reflect the world in complex and myriad ways: 'not a supposedly bare reality, but rather the contradictory ensemble of its representations, an ensemble which can only be aptly designated by the concept of ideology, undoubtedly a most contentious concept' (Macherey, 2006, 363). Marx thinks that ideology is part of the superstructure: the conventions and cultures that form the dominant ideas of society. Crucially, to say that texts reflect these ideas does not always mean literature tactility supports the status quo. As we will see in the Maupassant story, texts can challenge and subvert dominant ideas.

Maupassant is one of the most sophisticated practitioners of the short story. He survived his military service in the Franco-Prussian War (1870–1871) and wrote hundreds of darkly comic stories. For Marxist critics, texts bear the direct imprint of historical circumstances, meaning that Maupassant's works are a compendium of complex and contradictory desires related to the circumstances of his own time, such as hapless marriages, the struggle for social approval, and the desire and attainment of luxury. Crucially, Maupassant has been less critically regarded because he occupies a historical moment shortly before the significance of Freud, the introspective, self-analytical mood of Proust, and the development of the novel as the dominant form of literary expression.

'The Necklace' features a disgruntled individual, Madame Loisel, 'a pretty, charming young woman born into a working-class family, as if by some accident of fate' (Maupassant, 2009, 168). Stuck in her class position, Madame Loisel had 'no dowry, no hopes, no way of becoming famous, understood, loved or the wife of a rich distinguished man' (*ibid.*). As such, she is forced to marry a loving yet lowly ranked clerk – masculine failure is a staple of the Maupassant short story – and lives a deeply unhappy life, without fine clothes or expensive jewelry. (Capitalist society revels in the false gratification of luxury items and indulgent consumerism.) One day, her husband receives an invitation to a ministerial party. A successful performance of taste and class will, she hopes, translate into economic advancement and greater social status. Lamenting that she has nothing to wear, Madame Loisel refuses to attend. Her husband, in an act of charity, bestows upon her 400 francs that he was saving for himself, which she uses to purchase a dress. She then borrows an expensive diamond necklace from an acquaintance. On leaving the party, the couple discover that the necklace is lost. An exhaustive search reveals nothing, meaning the pair must replace the necklace by buying a similar one in a boutique. They take on debts and commit to lengthy repayments. They endure abject poverty, physical deprivation, and moral torment for ten years, until, at last, all the debts are paid. Then one day, while walking along the Champs-Élysées, Madame Loisel encounters her friend. She admits the years of hard labour and all that she has sacrificed to fund the return of the necklace. In a terrible twist – a Maupassant specialty – the original necklace is revealed as a fake, worth a minor sum.

ANALYSIS

How can we use Marx's ideas to think about this text? As we have already suggested, there is no single approach, but there are critical perspectives on common themes. We might begin with class, and class consciousness, suggesting that Madame Loisel feels the profound disparities of capitalism and wishes to change her class position. We are told she is unhappy as the wife of a clerk and dreams 'of fine dinners, of shining silverware, [...] of delicious dishes served on wonderful plates, of whispered gallantries listened to with an inscrutable smile as one ate the pink flesh of a trout or the wings of a quail' (*ibid.*). She feels the best way to do this is to accumulate social or cultural capital (that is, not so much material objects, although this is still important, but the cultivation of tastes, manners, skills, credentials that are believed to belong to a specific class). Wearing the necklace, she believes, will mark her out as a cultured, elegant, and wealthy woman. It signifies the values she wishes to be known for. Cultural capital is a performance of class desire.

We may then turn to the commodity, the necklace itself, which is a strange object. The necklace prompts a reflection on the distinction between value and price. The object is perceived as valuable because it is assumed to be an expensive luxury item. But where is this value? Is the value inherent in the object itself?

Or is value a social relation, one that we place upon the object? That the necklace is fake underscores this point thoroughly. We place great importance upon such objects under capitalism, but are these objects actually worth what we think they are worth?

It is not simply the case, however, that the text reflects Marxist themes, a situation in which we seek out points of comparison between the two, or more forcibly impose Marxist ideas on the text. The more fundamental question for Marxist critique is how the text can potentially develop and enrich critical approaches to literature with the aim of expanding its field of observation, influence, and relevance.

Other Marxist critics and philosophers have turned to this text. In *What is Literature?* Jean-Paul Sartre (1905–1980) reads the Maupassant short story as a kind of bourgeois social institution that exists to provide reassurance to the leisured and wealthy by keeping class categories intact. For Sartre, everything concurs in symbolising the stable bourgeoisie of the end of the century, who think that nothing more will happen, and who believe in the eternity of capitalist organisation (Sartre, 1988, 125–126). The Maupassant short story, at least for Sartre, is a vindication of capitalism by proposing that class categories exist to keep avaricious habits in check. The desire to move up a notch on the class ladder is presented as a form of transgression, and Madame Loisel is punished for her greed, shallowness, and untruth. If she did not wish to have luxury items, then, we might say, none of this would have happened. The story reveals the contradictions of late-nineteenth-century French bourgeoise society, acting as a scathing critique of social class, and the monstrous power of capital and commodities to determine human existence.

SUMMARY

As I have argued in this chapter, Marx's preface to *A Contribution to the Critique of Political Economy* is a remarkably rich document. One of the central ideas discussed in the preface is the base and superstructure. Marx's idea of the relationship between economic phenomena and social, cultural, and political infrastructure is nuanced and complex. For Marx, the sum of the forces and relations of production in each society constitute its 'base', which is firstly a fundamental reality. From the base there develops a 'superstructure', which comprises all other aspects of the social, cultural, and political life of that given society. Several contemporary Marxist intellectuals have challenged, extended, and developed these ideas, arguing for the necessity to rethink the relationship between culture and economics by moving beyond readings that emphasise prediction and control. Using the work of contemporary Marxist thinkers, we can understand the base and superstructure relation more as a problem to be discussed and resolved in new historical contexts, rather than as a blanket approach to all present and future societies.

7

HISTORY

Leo Tolstoy's (1828–1910) *War and Peace* (1867) is the most famous historical novel. Beginning in 1805, it follows the French invasion of Russia and the Napoleonic Wars, covering the lives of five Russian aristocratic families across its 1,500 pages. Originally published in serial format, the final instalment came out in 1867, the same year that Marx published *Capital*. If Marx's subject was a critique of capital (to lay bare the laws of motion that govern the capitalist mode of production), then Tolstoy's was history. As Isaiah Berlin argues,

> Tolstoy's interest in history and the problem of historical truth was passionate, almost obsessive, both before and during the writing of *War and Peace*. No one who reads his journals and letters, or indeed *War and Peace* itself, can doubt that the author himself, at any rate, regarded this problem as the heart of the entire matter – the central issue round which the novel is built.
>
> (Berlin, 2013, 442)

Tolstoy wanted to discover and formulate a set of laws of history that would explain human development. *War and Peace* is this effort. The novel constantly juxtaposes reality with what 'really' occurred, showing a distinction between official accounts and personal experience. In Tolstoy's novel, history is given an inner and outer texture.

Marx, too, had views on history. Like Tolstoy, he was not interested in knowing about the past simply for its own sake. Nor did he subscribe to what is often called the "Great Man" theory of history, put forward by the conservative writer Thomas Carlyle (1795–1881), which argues that great leaders make the world. Marx dismissed this kind of history as 'high sounding dramas about princes and states', as it glossed over the contributions of other classes (Marx and Engels, 1970, 57). The German poet Bertolt Brecht (1898–1956) captures this when he writes: 'Who built the seven gates of Thebes? / The Books are filled with names of Kings. / Was it Kings who hauled the craggy blocks of stone?' (Brecht, 1987, 252). Marx was interested in those who did the hard work. He set out to grasp the specific social forms of material production, the struggles of workers, and the structures governing societies.

Marx never used the term 'historical materialism' (it was used by Engels), but he did labour to understand the vast historical shifts taking place in his lifetime. The world that Marx inherited and lived in was anything but stable. Revolutions toppled apparently well established political regimes, and these events had a powerful impact on Marx. In a range of texts, he argued that history proceeds through a series of modes of production, characterised by class struggles that culminate in the breakdown of capitalism and the emergence of communism. The result, however, was not inevitable: one could not sit back and simply wait for technology and economic development to create a new society by themselves. This was the forceful, dramatic conclusion of the eleventh thesis of Feuerbach – 'the philosophers have only interpreted the world in various ways; the point is to change it' – emblazoned on Marx's grave in London (Marx, *MECW5*, 5). Communism could be achieved only by political struggle.

Marx, then, had a philosophy of history, but he was also important for two other reasons. First, he was a historian and wrote incisively about events taking place in his lifetime. Second, he was a major historical figure, forever associated with criticising capitalism, arguing for communism, and advancing revolution. Marx's analysis of capitalism was deemed so important that, for Louis Althusser, Marx had founded a new science. Marx, argued Althusser, had discovered History – a new 'continent' of Knowledge – in the same way that Sigmund Freud (1856–1939) had discovered psychoanalysis (Althusser, 2005, 14). For Althusser, Marx's political economy was all about uncovering the long-term structural dynamics at work in human history. In discovering modes of production, economic exchange, and class struggles, Marx had specified the course of future human development and set out a new science of society. These arguments were compelling in their time, but we should be wary of reading Marx too forcefully.

Marx's thought is deeply, profoundly historical. Hegel had taught Marx that history was constant change, full of conflicts, oppositions, and contradictions. Hegel was the first philosopher to develop a detailed theory that claimed to have discovered a meaning or direction to history. History, thought Hegel, 'is the process where the Spirit discovers itself and its own concept' (Hegel, 1975, 62). But Marx thought that Hegel had mistaken the real force of history. History was not the conflict of ideas, but the conflict of classes. This was not Marx's idea. Other historians had already arrived at this conclusion. What Marx added was a materialist theory of historical change that saw human agency as the crucial factor, but with this agency always in dialogue with powerful external forces and pressures that could not be controlled because they were inherited. 'Men make their own history', Marx wrote – meaning, of course, humanity – 'but they do not make it as they please; they do not make it under self-selected circumstances, but under circumstances existing already, given and transmitted from the past' (Marx, 2019, 480).

Marx brought to history and class struggle a radical conception of how it would end. Political economists such as David Ricardo (1772–1823) were convinced that capitalism could continue indefinitely, reaching an equilibrium between the conflicting interests of capitalists and workers. Marx disagreed, believing that greater quantities of wealth would accumulate in the hands of few capitalists and create the social conditions ripe for revolution. He also thought that as capitalism spread across the globe, it would run up against the limits of the natural world (such as land and resources). Technological advances would mean that, over time, the rate of profit would decline. Towards the end of his life, he thought that capitalism could be surpassed without violent revolution in some countries (such as the United States) and that not every society would have to pass through the same sequence of historical stages. But that capitalism would be replaced by communism was, for Marx, never in doubt.

Marx connects history to politics, economics, and ideology. As I argued in 'Why Marx?', Marx conceives of everything within a specific socio-economic formation, or mode of production, where class is a central category of social analysis. History for Marx is simply a term, it:

> does nothing, it 'possesses no immense wealth', it 'wages no battles'. It is man, real, living man who does all that, who possesses and fights: 'history' is not, as it were, a person apart, using man as a means to achieve its own aims, history is nothing but the activity of man pursuing his aims.
>
> (Marx, *MECW4*, 93)

It was not history but humanity that was central. Marx wanted to keep the focus on the activities of men and women as they engaged in constant, active, struggle under capitalist conditions of exploitation. For Marx, history is not a chronicle of past events but a story of human freedom.

Marx studied history to create a better future. His unique contribution was to bring together nature, social relations, and praxis (self-creating activity). For Marx, capitalism had reduced humans to productive activity. For Marx, productive practices, long ignored by religion and philosophy, are in fact 'achingly central to what we are' (Pendakis *et al.*, 2018, xxi). This has always posed the question of whether Marx shifted the locus of intelligibility from that of individuals to structures. Althusser certainly thought this, asking Marxists to concentrate on ideology and the system of relationships in dynamic articulation. Such a reading raised a good deal of controversy, meaning most Marxists today are disposed to meet somewhere in the middle, empathising the importance of individual acts within the structure of capital. This appears closer to Marx's original position, when he writes that 'Men make their own history but they do not make it as they please; they do not make it under self-selected circumstances, but under circumstances existing already, given and transmitted from the past' (Marx, 2010, 146). The whole thrust of Marx's political writings is that individuals can change the conditions which they inherit through action. Situations do not determine individuals completely, but they do influence them in significant ways.

Marx's writings on history often provide detailed readings of circumstances and conditions, such as the 1851 French *coup d'état*, but imbued with a desire for social and economic justice. Marx himself claims he does not fall 'into the error of our so-called *objective* historians' but approaches history with an eye towards human potential and individual self-realisation (Marx, 2019, 478). He does not just seek a general understanding of history, but reads in historical events decisive features for future political struggles. Marx focuses on liberating individuals from modern industrial capitalism as a condition of human flourishing in some future social phase called communism. To do this without a critique of social structures, however, would be impossible, hence Marx's immersion in political economy. Marx's most important writings on history are the *Communist Manifesto*, *The German Ideology*, *The Class Struggles in France 1848 to 1850*, *The Eighteenth Brumaire of Louis Bonaparte*, and selected chapters of *Capital* dealing with the historical emergence of capitalists and proletarians. We can only examine some of these works here.

Marx's whirlwind descriptions of changes wrought by capital encapsulate the force and flux of history in what can only be described as a powerful communist poetics. But to turn from Marx's writings of the 1840s to those of the 1850s is to move from the abstract exhortations of the *Communist Manifesto* to correspondingly concrete forms of historical analysis. It is worth reminding ourselves that the forms that Marx chooses to write in – whether political manifesto, journalistic article, or long-form essay – entail formal limits and sometimes demand simplification as a matter of strategy. Despite this, the sheer range of connections that Marx makes in the *Manifesto* reveal his ability to blend deep historical insight with a critical attitude towards communism.

The revolutions of 1848 had a huge significance for Marx. First, they revealed the existence of strong, independent, working-class political movements in Europe, and the beginning of the modern socialist movement. Second, they formed an opportunity for Marx to reflect upon his social and political theories in relation to events occurring. France, in particular, had ushered in sudden and dramatic transformations, and, coupled with the relatively undeveloped character of French capitalism, provided Marx with rich and representative material for his studies. Political revolutions dominated Marx's life, and he was acutely aware of the ways in which such momentous shifts made themselves felt for members of his own generation.

Marx wrote two short books on the revolutions of 1848: *The Class Struggles in France 1848 to 1850* and *The Eighteenth Brumaire of Louis Bonaparte*. The former first appeared in the *Neue Rheinische Zeitung: Organ der Demokratie*, a daily newspaper that had a good circulation in Germany amongst political emigrés. Engels called *The Class Struggles in France* 'Marx's first attempt to explain a section of contemporary society by means of [the] materialist conception' (Engels, *MECW27*, 506). For Engels, Marx attempted to 'demonstrate the inner causal connection [...] to trace political events back to effects of what were, in the final analysis, economic causes' rather than 'interpret political events of the day' (*ibid.*). For Engels, Marx had achieved a rare thing, having 'worked out anew the history of France from February 1848' (*ibid.*). Marx does examine class structures and economic relations, but it is also the political factions and cliques of the bourgeoise that catch his concern. This interest with French affairs continues with *The Eighteenth Brumaire*, in which Marx accounts for how the revolutions of 1848 led to the *coup d'état* of December 1851. *The Eighteenth Brumaire* was planned to appear in instalments in *Die Revolution*, published in the USA, but the periodical fell through. The text finally appeared in May 1852.

While *The Class Struggles in France* and *The Eighteenth Brumaire* tend to be treated as works of history – specifically French history – they nevertheless raise enduring theoretical questions about the state, class conflict, and ideology through a nuanced grasp of historical background and an impressive, powerful command of language. Marx had followed the development of the revolutions from London, but by mid-1850 he knew they were at an end. Marx thought the next political outbreak would come with the future economic crisis, meaning that, at least for now, capital would need to develop more substantially. Members of the central committee of the Communist League were arrested in Cologne in May 1851, and the London branch subsequently crumbled. Marx started a defence campaign for the Cologne Communist prisoners who were tried in October 1852, and wrote an indictment of the case and the Prussian police force titled *Revelations Concerning the Communist Trial in Cologne* (1853). Despite the campaign, most members were sentenced to prison and the League was later dissolved. Largely removed from political affairs, Marx turned to reading and the continuation of his studies in political economy.

THE CLASS STRUGGLES IN FRANCE 1848 TO 1850

In the *Communist Manifesto*, Marx had claimed simpler class antagonisms. Chiefly for the purposes of impressing communism on the political imagination, Marx had argued that there were two fundamental classes characteristic of industrial capitalism: the bourgeoise and the proletariat, or the worker and the capitalist. He provisionally provided an essentialist foundation, or binary, as a strategy for collective representation and empowerment. In *The Class Struggles in France*, he complicated this perspective.

The Class Struggles in France is a set of articles later collated and republished by Engels after Marx's death. Like the *Communist Manifesto*, they are lively texts, brimming with Marx's incisive analysis and characteristic flair. In them, for the first time, Marx begins to develop a detailed set of concepts for understanding the course of class struggle. In the 1850s, Marx was still invested in questions of political strategy, and here he sensed an opportunity for revolutionary change.

The history of work and workers in France has several unique features that make the national situation more complex. French society was made up of a rich variety of class factions, each with a different allegiance to a different political party. Wealthy land-owners, financial workers, industry owners, coupled with factory workers, farmers, and small peasant proprietors, all complicated any strict separation of class interest. 'The struggle in its highly developed modern form', wrote Marx, 'at its crucial point, the struggle of the industrial wage labourer against the industrial bourgeoise – is in France a partial phenomenon' (Marx, 2019, 380). This meant that industrial production existed alongside other modes of production – such as peasant or artisan pro-duction, which had its own tradition, culture, and ideologically constituted structure. In *The Class Struggles in France*, Marx qualified his original position identifying a single ruling class to reflect the complexity of class formation, interest, and struggle in post-revolutionary France. The revolutionary strategy Marx defends in 1850 is all about the worker's ability to act and imple-ment change.

The American author Thomas Pynchon (1937–) is concerned with history. As a postmodern author, Pynchon treats history as a theme park: a place of thrill-seeking, wild rides, and exhilarating entertainment. For Pynchon, history is a subjunctive space: a place of openness and desirability where fantastical solutions exist to political problems. In *Mason & Dixon* (1997), the reader confronts a supernatural world that capitalist America will soon devour. It is a place 'where golems stalk the land, mechanized ducks fly, men transform into magical creatures, and vegetables can house whole families' (Carswell, 2017, 15). Pynchon refuses to let the past become a settled space, showing how every moment contains a radical potential. 'Facts are but the Play-things of lawyers [...] Tops and Hoops, forever a-spin' – forming not 'a Chain of single Links', but rather 'a great disorderly Tangle of Lines, long and short, weak and strong, vanishing into the Mnemonick Deep, with only their Destination in common.' (Pynchon, 1997, 349). Turning the past into a space of adven-ture is an effort to locate the elusive 'singular point in American history' where 'we jumped the wrong way', and in *Gravity's Rainbow* (1973) becomes an attempt to find 'the fork in the road America never took'. (Pynchon, 2000, 556).

POSTMODERNISM

Postmodernism is an artistic movement that began in the middle of the twentieth century, after the end of the Second World War (1945), and lasted until the 1990s, spanning literature, culture, film, theory, and architecture. As the name suggests, it occurs as a reaction to modernism. It employs a mixing of high and low cultures, a distrust of traditional narrative modes (such as realism), and a self-reflexive acknowledgement of its status as a constructed aesthetic artefact. In literature, postmodern novels tend to draw the reader's attention to the fact that they are reading a work of fiction through devices that shatter the illusion of an all-encompassing fictional world. In Brett Easton Ellis's *American Psycho* (1991), the reader is never sure if Patrick Bateman's violent acts are real (within the novel) or the bizarre hallucinations of a psychopathic imagination. Key postmodern authors include Paul Auster, Douglas Copeland, Don DeLillo, Kurt Vonnegut, Thomas Pynchon, Toni Morrison, and Katherine Dunn. Theorists of Postmodernism include Jean Francois Lyotard, Jean Baudrillard, and Fredric Jameson.

MARX AND *THE EIGHTEENTH BRUMAIRE OF LOUIS BONAPARTE*

Perhaps Marx's most famous pronouncement on history is in *The Eighteenth Brumaire*. The term *Brumaire* refers to the second month in the French Republican Calendar, the date of the end of the first Revolution in 1799. First published in parts in a German monthly magazine, the text was written between December 1851 and March 1852, and is considered by some historians to be Marx's finest work of political analysis. It examines Louis-Napoléon Bonaparte's sudden seizing of power in France in 1851, and contrasts this political crisis with the earlier revolution in France. But Marx wrote the text to explain why the 1848 revolutions in Paris had led to Bonaparte assuming dictatorial powers only a few years later. Marx considered Louis Napoléon to be a poor figure when compared to his uncle, the revolutionary and Hegelian hero Napoléon Bonaparte (1769–1821). *The Eighteenth Brumaire* is colourful, extravagant, and untidy, leading Terrell Carver to remark that it is 'the closest Marx could get to the movies', and that 'the genre is that of the docu-drama, in which factual reportage merges with political performance' (Carver, 2003, 8). The opening is among Marx's most frequently quoted comments. Marx describes how the heroes of the French Revolution enacted profound historical changes in Roman dress, while those of the English Civil War were in the guise of Old Testament prophets. Marx's point here is that such bourgeoise revolutions are prosaic, at odds with the high seriousness of the political moment. They require costume and dress to grant them an emotional charge. Further, repetitions of bourgeoise revolutions, as Marx's qualification of Hegel suggests, evoke not heroism but farce:

> Hegel remarks somewhere that all great world-historic facts and personages appear, so to speak, twice. He forgot to add: the first time as tragedy, the second time as farce. Caussidière for Danton, Louis Blanc for Robespierre, the Montagne of 1848 to 1851 for the Montagne of 1793 to 1795, the nephew for the uncle. And the same caricature occurs in the circumstances of the second edition of the Eighteenth Brumaire.
>
> (Marx, 2019, 480)

Such was Marx's reading of the situation of Napoleon III. Two paintings reveal this stark contrast: Jacques-Louis David's *Napoleon Crossing the Alps* (1801) shows a figure of world historical significance, astride a horse and leading troops into battle; *The Emperor Napoleon III* (1853) by Franz Xaver Winterhalter reveals all the dress and deportment of a largely discredited monarchy.

This is central to Marx's reading of the revolutions of 1848, which were efforts to re-enact the original French revolution some 50 years earlier. Most obviously, Marx had demonstrated that the working class could play a revolutionary part. Although the period after the revolution led to reaction in the figure of Bonaparte, French workers would be able to reveal their collective strength again.

THE GERMAN IDEOLOGY

To claim that this text contains a materialist conception of history would be to invoke the wrath of Marx himself, who claimed in his preface to *A Contribution to the Critique of Political Economy* that *The German Ideology* was best left to 'the gnawing criticism of the mice' (Marx, 1992, 427). Interestingly, the expression 'a materialist conception of history' is not present in the text, with Marx and Engels speaking rather of 'practical materialists' and 'a communist materialist' among similar and like-minded terms (*MECW5*, 38, 41). As Massimiliano Tomba argues, historical materialism, as a theory of history or a materialist conception of history, does not exist. But this comes with a qualification – it is not because there is no theory of history in *The German Ideology*, but rather because Marx and Engels never deploy this term (Tomba, 2013, vii). There is certainly a distinctive conception of history here, but not the kind that has been promulgated with the codified tradition of 'historical materialism'. As George Tomlinson has argued, there is here a 'distinctive conception of history – one consistent with "the materialist outlook" – which can be articulated as a concept – a philosophical concept – of history in more rich and nuanced ways' (Tomlinson, 2015, 2). This striking realisation requires us to consider the text in more constructive and critical modes, but also to reflect, albeit briefly, on a question I cannot fully answer here – How is it that an untitled set of incoherent fragments, the original manuscript unnumbered and filled with deletions, corrections, and marginalia, written in the 1840s and abandoned by their authors, achieved canonical status and came to represent Marx's world historical outlook?

MARXIST HISTORIOGRAPHY

Marx's writings on history were often incisive and engaging critical studies of world historical events. His focus on class, struggle, and revolution, along with the general spirit of his critique, were powerfully developed in twentieth-century Marxism, which pioneered a rich tradition of historical interpretation. Eric Hobsbawm (1917–2012), perhaps the most renowned historian of the twentieth century, produced an astonishing body of work, including a four-volume world history (*The Age of Revolution, The Age of Capital, The Age of Empire, The Age of Extremes*) that began with the revolutions in France and ended with the disintegration of the Soviet Union. The British historian E.P. Thompson set out to 'rescue the poor stockinger, the Luddite cropper, and the "obsolete" hand-loom weaver' in *The Making of the English Working Class* (1963), while Howard Zinn, in *A People's History of the United States* (1980), renounced the legacy of American triumphalism to present the lives of those engaged in fighting slavery, labour struggles, and working class socialism (Thompson, 1980, 12). Comparable efforts were made in the fields of literature and popular culture by Stuart Hall and Raymond Williams. Most of these efforts were concerned with 'history from below', focusing on the neglected narratives of the working class, and drawing upon Marx's theory of history.

SUMMARY

What are often categorised as Marx's historical texts are really a collection of critical approaches that encompass class, communism, and history. In Marx's historical writings – including the *Communist Manifesto*, *The German Ideology*, *The Class Struggles in France 1848 to 1850*, *The Eighteenth Brumaire of Louis Bonaparte*, and sections of *Capital*, Marx examines the independence of the state from class interests, the plurality of class formations, and the determining power of ideas and imagery in politics – concerns that are not readily associated with Marx's materialist outlook. After the defeat of the 1848 revolutions, and with the subsequent economic crisis of the 1850s, Marx moved away from political activity to concentrate on *Capital*.

8

CLASS

What class are you? In thinking about this question, you will probably reflect on your social, cultural, and economic circumstances. You will likely think about your annual income, whether you own property, and if you have any savings. You may consider your status within society in relation to your occupation (coffee barista, hedge-fund manager, undergraduate student). Finally, you might reflect on the range of cultural activities you enjoy, like visiting art galleries, playing video games, or listening to jazz. These are simply some of the questions that were asked by the BBC in the Great British Class Survey. Launched in 2011, the survey received over 160,000 responses and identified seven different classes, including 'an elite, whose wealth separates them from an established middle class, as well as a class of technical experts and a class of "new affluent" workers' (Savage, 2015). The Great British Class Survey pointed to new kinds of class stratification in its examination of social, cultural, and economic capital.

Class has a very different meaning for Marx. In the examples given above – in economics and sociology – class is a designation of different social groups based on factors including status, income, and culture. For Marx, class structures are essential to understanding capitalism and creating revolutionary change. Class, at least for Marx, is a social relationship rather than a fixed position or rank in society (the capitalist class could not exist without the proletariat, and *vice versa*). In the *Communist Manifesto*, which I examined in Chapter Three, Marx argues that the relationship between classes in capitalism is uneven, antagonistic, and involves conflict. Sadly, Marx never provided an exact or precise definition of social class (the *Communist Manifesto* is a political document where Marx does not wish to get bogged down in long explanations; the manuscript of *Capital* Volume 3, where Marx discusses social class, is incomplete and breaks off). However, Marx's theory suggests that class is a deeply political relation, it is the 'collective expression of the fact of exploitation, the way exploitation is embedded in the social structure' of capitalism. (de Ste Croix, 1983, 43). Crucially, 'individuals constituting a given class may or may not be wholly or partially conscious of their own identity and common interests as a class, and they may or may not feel antagonism towards members of other classes as such' (*ibid.*, 44). Members of the working class may not be fully aware of how they are exploited by capitalists, but this does not alter the fact of exploitation.

Marx treats classes in objective terms, in respect to their relationship to private property and the means of production (the bourgeoise own factories; the proletariat have only labour power). Subjective factors, such as taste, manners, likes and dislikes, are less important for Marx. Indeed, these are often not freely chosen activities but expressions of class interests, with Marx arguing in *The German Ideology* that the 'ideas of the ruling class are in every epoch the ruling ideas: i.e., the class which is the ruling material force of society is at the same time its ruling intellectual force' (*MECW5*, 59). For Marx, classes have meaning to the extent that they are opposed, in conflict with other classes. Classes are defined by the antagonistic nature of capitalist social relations, which for Marx must ultimately be ended to achieve human freedom.

In this chapter, I will start by explaining the importance and relevance of class in contemporary culture, before discussing three core concepts in relation to Marx's key ideas on class. First, I will examine different classes in capitalism. Second, I will turn to class conflict (sometimes called class struggle), which Marx's considers to be the motor force of history and historical change.

Third, I will turn to the situation of the worker as represented in Marx's *Capital*, where he examines economic relations in their broadest political significance. Using recent examples from literature and film, I will show how Marx's ideas can elucidate our present situation under global capitalism.

It is important to note from the outset that Marx did not invent the concept of social class, but it did become central to his politics and political philosophy.

GLOBAL INEQUALITY AND THE RETURN OF CLASS

As long as there is class division and social inequality, Marx will be relevant. But there is an assumption, often promoted by those who tend to deny class conflict, that Marx's idea about class and class struggle only correspond to a world of 'factories and food riots, coal miners and chimney sweeps, widespread misery and massed working classes' (Eagleton, 2011, 1). We now inhabit a flexible, global, post-industrial world where free markets mean that global poverty is decreasing. Social unrest and political agitation are no longer needed, caused only by malcontents who envy the wealthy. Put simply, such proponents argue that Marx is a nineteenth-century thinker whose views no longer apply to the working class as it is currently constituted.

But this can hardly be true in a world where exploitation still exists, and where one country owns 30 per cent of the world's total wealth. Marx spoke about the development of industrial capitalism, but he also spoke about an uneven, class-divided world. Today, according to UNICEF, some 26,000 children die each day in the poorest villages in the world. One in six people do not have access to clean water. Millions of women spend hours in back-breaking toil drawing water, collecting wood, or searching for food. Over 2 billion people – that is, those lucky enough to have food – rely on colleting firewood to cook an evening meal. Marx first addressed this situation in his articles on the criminalisation of wood gathering, published in the *Rheinische Zeitung* in the 1840s. There are striking continuities here, and at least from this perspective, Marx's focus on the real struggles of the peasants is a broad contention about what links humans in the end: the presence of suffering, the reality of historical oppression, and an enduring desire for freedom (Pendakis *et al.*, 2018, xxiii). Marx was fully aware that classes are not fixed entities, and that the pace and intensity of organised class struggle and social protest movements are subject to development and change. In what follows, I will give a brief examination of Marxist-inflected approaches to social class, to show why Marx's ideas on class and class struggle are more relevant than ever.

Marx's theory of class, and broader forms of class critique, have only recently returned. In the 1980s, in the United Kingdom and the United States, class was delegitimised through an aggressive 'Thatcherite' rhetoric of class denial. Moral character and personal capacity replaced economic processes as explanations for individual agency, leading some scholars to assert that 'class as a concept is ceasing to do any useful work', or even more stridently proclaiming the 'death of class' (Pakulski and Waters, 1995). One commentator even boasted that the United States has no classes, and that workers do not significantly share distinct, life-defining experiences (Kingston, 2001). After the 2008 financial crisis and subsequent austerity measures, there has been a concerted effort to shift sentiments of anger, panic, and moral outrage towards the working class. The 'effects of austerity are felt differently across the income distribution. Those at the bottom of the income distribution lose more than those at the top for the simple reason that those at the top rely far less on government-produced services and can afford to lose more because they have more wealth to start with' (Blyth, 2013, 8). Austerity was claimed as a common-sense solution to the financial crisis, but it is a class-based project for cutting debt.

The journalist Owen Jones has focused on efforts by the mainstream media to justify increasing social inequality by attempts to recast the working class as feckless and feral. For Jones, the construction of a social underclass, or 'chav culture', is a demonisation of the working class (Jones, 2012). In a similar vein, Frances Ryan has explored the ways in which politicians and tabloid newspapers have mounted a conscious campaign against those seeking support for living with disabilities. For Ryan, these attacks are part of an effort to dismantle welfare reforms by portraying those with complex needs as scroungers and benefit cheats (Ryan, 2019). And David Stuckler and Sanjay Basu extensively catalogue the consequences of the financial crisis and austerity measures on the health and wellbeing of global populations. The failure to fund social protection programmes – such as healthcare, mental health counselling, disability allowance and housing, all deemed too expensive in a time of national debt – has caused higher death rates (Stuckler and Basu, 2013).

Marx would have supported the spirit of this critique. But he believed that, under capitalism, workers retained the potential to become active agents of political change. As we saw in Chapter Three, in the *Communist Manifesto* Marx argued that society was splitting up into two great hostile camps: bourgeoisie and proletariat. Importantly, Marx is not suggesting that it has always been this way. He is referring to capitalist social relations, meaning that for long periods before the emergence and development of capitalism, classes did not exist. People lived to hunt and gather food, living in small communities that moved across the land. Hierarchies still existed, in and between tribes, but these are not the same as classes. This was called a 'primitive communism' where 'production was essentially collective' and 'consumption preceded by direct distribution of the products within larger or small communistic communities' (Engels, 1972, 233). There was no real interest in private property because goods were usually shared among the group, meaning wealth was too difficult to accumulate. In the following section, I will turn to Marx's understanding of classes under capitalism in greater detail.

CLASSES UNDER CAPITALISM

The main classes under capitalism are the bourgeoisie and proletariat. Other classes exist for Marx, such as landlords, petty bourgeoise (small-scale merchants), peasants, and the *lumpenproletariat* (the lower orders of society without revolutionary potential), but they are not primary in terms of the dynamics of capitalist development. For Marx, the bourgeoisie are the owners of capital, purchasing and exploiting labour power, and using the surplus value (the added value raised from the sale of a product) to accumulate or expand their capital. Today they appear slightly different from the factory owners Marx attacked in *Capital*. The wars between labour and capital that Marx dramatised in that book have their parallel in the best works of nineteenth-century literature. Charles Dickens (1812–1870) had experience of these hardships while working in a blacking factory, and went after zealous capitalists in texts including *The Old Curiosity Shop* (1840), *Little Dorrit* (1857), and *The Pickwick Papers* (1836). In *Hard Times* (1854), Dickens criticises the poor living conditions of the working class in industrial towns, using a fictional place – 'Coketown' – as representative of the exploitation, desperation, and oppression of the workers who slave in the factories. The descriptions of the factory are especially grim, but the most powerful critique is ideological, in the form of the capitalist class's lack of empathy and belief that workers are feckless, lazy, and insufficiently self-interested:

> Any capitalist … who had made sixty thousand pounds out of sixpence, always professed to wonder why the sixty thousand nearest Hands didn't each make sixty thousand pounds out of sixpence, and more or less reproached them every one for not accomplishing the little feat. What I did you can do. Why don't you go and do it?
>
> (Dickens, 2003, 124).

Vicious factory owners still exist, but modern manufacturing has moved to the poor periphery. Contemporary Chinese fiction is, in many ways, dealing with similar issues to those explored by Dickens. Marx was aware of this suffering in developing countries, and there is abundant evidence that factories in China recreate the conditions that Marx described in nineteenth-century England.

Today, capitalists tend to belong among the major shareholders of corporations, boards of directors, and chief executive officers. They are surrounded by a bureaucracy that organises the exploitation of workers, the sale of products and services, and keeps a surplus portion of the labour from others. Crucially, then, they are defined by their role in the exploitation of labour and the desire to expand their individual capital. To be wealthy is, in itself, not sufficient to be a capitalist. It is the active use of wealth towards self-expansion through the employment and exploitation of workers to generate profit that counts. Marx was writing when industrial capital was beginning to emerge, but his ideas apply equally to the world of twenty-first-century financial capitalism, where class structures still exist. After the 2008 financial crash, several films, documentaries, and TV series about global finance began to appear. *Wall Street: Money Never Sleeps* (2010), *Inside Job* (2010), *Too Big to Fail* (2011), *Margin Call* (2011), *The Wolf of Wall Street* (2013), *The Big Short* (2015), and *Billions* (2016) all fostered debate about greed and the unchecked power of corporate capitalism.

The movie drama *Margin Call* (Chandor, 2011) is the best, exploring class, capitalism, and investment fraud in a critical manner, set over one day at a successful Wall Street investment bank. A risk analyst discovers problems with the firm's portfolio of financial assets. A late-night meeting takes place at which the company decides to sell all its assets, spreading risk throughout the market and unleashing the financial crisis. In a key moment in the film, the CEO of the bank, John Tuld, talks about the history of capitalist crisis, saying: 'It's all just the same thing over and over; we can't help ourselves. And you and I can't control it, or stop it, or even slow it. Or even ever-so-slightly alter it. We just react.' For Tuld, 'there have always been and there always will be the same percentage of winners and losers. Happy foxes and sad sacks. Fat cats and starving dogs in this world. Yeah, there may be more of us today than there's ever been. But the percentages? They stay exactly the same' (*ibid.*). These comments are a justification of capitalism. They are ideological: as quoted above, the 'ideas of the ruling class are in every epoch the ruling ideas' (*MECW5*, 59). For Tuld, the world is simply the way it is, and nothing can be done to change it. 'Money' Tuld remarks – in an echo of Mr Wednesday in Chapter Four – is 'made up. Pieces of paper with pictures on it so we don't have to kill each other just to get something to eat. It's not wrong. And it's certainly no different today than its ever been.' Capitalist crisis has been going on so long, it is natural: '1637, 1797, 1819, 37, 57, 84, 1901, 07, 29, 1937, 1974, 1987 – Jesus, didn't that fuck up me up good – 92, 97, 2000 and whatever we want to call this' (Chandor, 2011).

Margin Call focuses on investment bankers, capturing the greed, brutality, and ambivalence of financial capitalism. Most importantly, it shows that the actions of the characters are dependent on objective social processes, on the harsh realities of global capitalism. It is a film about the capitalist class, but there is one telling moment where we see what Marx would call a member of the proletariat. In one scene, two investment bankers step into an elevator. Between them is a cleaner, a low-wage worker. The whole scene is one of pretence, acknowledging the worker, stuck between the two bankers, without referring to her. The scene is symbolic of Marx's comments on class structures in capitalism. Workers 'belong not to this or that capitalist, but to the capitalist class' (Marx, 1978, 205). The proletariat are distinguished as the owners of labour power. They have no resources other than their ability to work, whether with their hands or minds. As they do not own property (which for Marx is the means of production, such as factories), to survive they must obtain wages for themselves and often for their family. This guarantees working for a capitalist in an exploitative social relationship.

Teddy Wayne's novel *Kapitoil* (2010) – a title blending capital, toil, and oil – powerfully captures class structures under neoliberal capitalism. Karim Issar, a young Qatarian computer scientist, develops a program he calls Kapitoil that allows profits to be gained by predicting fluctuations in the oil futures market. The success of Karim's program leads him to advance rapidly in his firm, but he experiences a moral conflict when he is faced with the choice of selling his program to his boss, or giving it away for free. He chooses to study biology, help to further his epidemiology project, and work in small store owned by his father.

There are, of course, a range of nineteenth- and twentieth-century novels concerned with the lives of the industrial working class. Alan Sillitoe's novel *Saturday Night and Sunday Morning* (1958) focuses on the industrial working class in Britain. It narrates the life of Arthur Seaton, a young working-class man who is engaged in monotonous factory employment.

CLASS AND STRUGGLE

As I have argued, Marx did not invent class, or class struggle. In a letter dated 5th March 1852, he writes that 'No credit is due to me for the discovering the existence of classes in modern society or the struggle between them. Long before me the bourgeois historians had described the historical development of this class struggle and bourgeoise economists, the economy of the classes' (*MECW25*, 268). What Marx did do, in his own view, was prove that the existence of classes is inextricable from historical phases in the development of production, that the class struggle necessarily leads to the dictatorship of the proletariat, and that this moment 'only constitutes the transition to the abolition of all classes and to a classless society' (*ibid.*, 268). For Marx, after the end of capitalism there occurs a limited transitory phase that leads to communism and to a classless society. Classes are linked to the stages of economic development, meaning that after capitalism, there will be no class distinctions. We must be careful with this comment: Marx is not suggesting distinctions no longer exist, but that with the disappearance of classes comes the end of repressive intuitions. There is a difference between Marx's democratic commitments and twentieth-century Marxism, which we will cover in more detail in Chapter Ten.

In the *Communist Manifesto*, Marx and Engels assert that the struggle between different classes – between the proletariat (workers) and the bourgeoise (owners of capital) – is the driving force of history. The opening lines proclaim that 'the history of all hitherto existing society is the history of class struggle' (Marx and Engels, 1998, 3). In an important correction to the original text, Engels clarified that 'the history of all hitherto existing society' referred to written history, and not to the primitive communities preceding the development of antagonistic class relations under capitalism. Both Marx and Engels recognised that, in earlier epochs, 'we find almost everywhere a complicated arrangement of society into various orders, a manifold gradation of social rank' (*ibid.*). They contrast this with the distinctive features of the bourgeoise epoch. With the development of industrial capitalism, complex class antagonisms are simplified: 'Society [is] more and more splitting into two great hostile camps, into two great classes directly facing each other' (*ibid.*).

The concept of class struggle is intended to capture the full spectrum of actions, practices, desires, and distributions operating within capitalism. It can refer both to large-scale demonstrations (strikes, riots, rebellions, revolutions, or occupations) and to everyday negotiations between workers and bosses on issues such as pay and working conditions. For instance, union workers may withdraw their labour, or go on strike, to enforce their interests against employers. As Barbara Foley argues, we need to keep in mind a wide understanding of such practices: 'When captured Africans jumped into the sea rather than endure the horrors of the Atlantic [slave trade] or enslaved women in the Caribbean committed infanticide, these two can be seen as instances – even when individual and desperate – of class struggle' (Foley, 2019, 4). For Marxists, class struggle captures the totality of the social relations of production, such as the nineteenth-century slave trade, in which racism finds its effectivity. The reality of class struggle is reflected at different levels of society, and implies that there is some resistance to exploitation, although the level of this resistance can vary. Even in periods of seeming social peace, class struggle is a daily reality.

In this sense, a novel by Toni Morrion (1931–2019), *Beloved* (1987), is a powerful example of class struggle. The novel is set shortly after the American Civil War (1861–1865) and inspired by a newspaper clipping about a fugitive slave, Margaret Garner, who killed her daughter rather than allow the child to return to slavery. Morrison found the news clipping in *The Black Book* (1974), which chronicles the lives of African Americans in the United States from slavery through the civil rights movement. Sethe, the protagonist of the novel, is an escaped slave from a plantation called 'Sweet Home'. Like Garner, Sethe kills her daughter, only for the child to return as a ghost and haunt the other characters. Sethe's escape, capture, and killing of her daughter (rather than have her returned to slavery) are all historically specific forms of African American class struggle. In *Beloved*, Morrison demonstrates racial, sexual, and class oppressions, showing that collective struggle against capitalism is the only viable solution for African Americans in white-dominated US society.

Before the *Communist Manifesto*, Engels had published *The Condition of the Working Class in England* (1845). In this book, he gave a harsh description of the bourgeois as 'a deeply demoralised class, incurably corrupted by selfishness, corroded in their very being' (Engels, 2009, xvii). Places such as Manchester and Birmingham, small towns a century before, had by the nineteenth century exploded into sprawling, thriving, and bustling industrial and commercial centres. Engels had first-hand experience of the lives of workers, and documented class conditions in his account. In contrast, Marx had a limited experience of the lives of working-class men and women. In *The Eighteenth Brumaire of Louis Bonaparte*, Marx confers names on the working class in relation to production. He produces a much-quoted list of those outside the normative structures of social ontology, that is, those who do not perform useful work:

> Alongside decayed roués of doubtful origin and uncertain means of subsistence, alongside ruined and adventurous scions of the bourgeoisie, there were vagabonds, discharged soldiers, discharged criminals, escaped galley slaves, swindlers, confidence tricksters, *lazzaroni*, pickpockets, sleight-of-hand experts, gamblers, *maquereaux*, brothel-keepers, porters, pen pushers, organ grinders, rag and bone merchants, knife grinders, tinkers, beggars: in short, the whole indeterminate, fragmented mass, tossed backwards and forwards
>
> (Marx, 2019, 531)

Marx considers the *lumpenproletariat* an impediment to the realisation of a classless society because they do not generate socially useful production. As beggars, prostitutes, and petty criminals, they form a reactionary class composed of outcasts who make up a section of the population of industrial centres.

MARX AND THE WORKER

In *Capital*, Marx considers economic relations, combining theoretical arguments with impassioned polemic. We have already discussed the ways in which Marx deploys art and literature to develop his critical vision. In *Capital*, characters are spoken of, but also speak for themselves. In one key passage, Marx writes in the voice of the worker:

> The capitalist therefore takes his stand [...] suddenly, however, there arises the voice of the worker, which had previously been stifled in the

sound and fury of the production process: 'The commodity I have sold you differs from the ordinary crowd of commodities in that its use creates value, a greater value than it costs. That is why you bought it [...] you and I know on the market only one law, that of the exchange of commodities.'

(Marx, 1990, 342–43).

Marx's personification of the worker (capital considers the worker a non-human) in 'Chapter 10: The Working Day' is a moment when Marx uses the voice of the proletariat to demand 'the value of my commodity' (*ibid.*, 343). In the preface to the first edition, Marx calls attention to the use of this device, instructing readers that an awareness of this trope should govern their reading of the text:

I do not by any means depict the capitalist and the landowner in rosy colours. But individuals are dealt with here only in so far as they are the personifications of economic categories, the bearers of particular class relations and interests. My standpoint [...] can less than any other make the individual responsible for relations whose creature he remains, socially speaking, however much he may subjectively raise himself above them.

(Marx, 1990, 92).

Marx's theatre of voices is immensely complex. For much of *Capital*, we are dealing with humans who are correlatives of impersonal economic processes.

WORKING-CLASS RESISTANCE

Marx's ideas have resonated with numerous writers. There are many powerful examples of novels, plays, and poems, often written by working-class authors, that present the diverse voices of working-class populations and the (forgotten) plight of workers under capitalism, and inspire hope for radical political change. John Steinbeck (1902–1968) wrote *The Grapes of Wrath* (1939), following the migration of the Joad family from their home in Oklahoma to the promised land of California. The Joads are sharecroppers, or tenant farmers: they do not own the land, but must give a part of the crop to the owner as a form of rent. The Joads are forced to migrate because the bank has foreclosed on the land. *The Grapes of Wrath* is a novel about the working class, advocating social reform by drawing attention to unfair working conditions and the difficulties facing migrants. It is also a 'cli-fi' novel, or climate fiction, portraying the ways in which the bank's greed has damaged a once rich and fertile land. It remains one of the most politically engaged fictions of the twentieth century.

The relationship between poetry and politics is made explicit in the work of Claude McKay (1889–1948). His poem, 'Johannesburg Mines', is short, simple, and direct, addressed to a middle-class audience presumably unfamiliar with the realities of working-class experience:

> In the Johannesburg mines
> There are 240,000 natives working.
> What kind of poem
> Would you make of that?

McKay's poem gives an exact figure about the number of natives working in the mines and challenges the reader to make art out of this information. The emotional impact of the poem is heightened by its brevity. As he doesn't detail the hardships experienced by the natives working in the mines, the reader is left to imagine them. It forges a connection between workers and reader.

In drama, *Waiting for Lefty* (1935) by Clifford Odets (1906–1963) is a powerful class-based approach to the New York taxi drivers' strike of 1934. Told in five acts, it is a masterpiece of agitprop theatre (combining political agitation and propaganda). The play uses short, brief, intense scenes, deploying chants and slogans for political impact. It blurs the boundaries between audience and actors (in the original production actors were sitting with the audience and shouted dialogue from their seats). The play uses character names as epithets: 'Lefty' is a left-wing leader of the Drivers' Union, while 'Fatt' is the overweight capitalist, living off the labour of the workers. The drama contains a direct political message (political revolution), turning the end of the play into a beginning: audience and actors become one single community, oriented towards action, as the play ends with an invocation to 'STRIKE, STRIKE, STRIKE!'. The play contains a reference to the *Communist Manifesto*, when the drivers are told, 'WORKERS OF THE WORLD' unite (*ibid.*).

SUMMARY

For Marx, class and class structures were central to understanding capitalism. While approaches in economics and sociology focus on class in relation to status, income, and culture, Marx understands class as a social relationship in conflict. This means that, for Marx, the ruling capitalist class could not exist without the proletariat, and *vice versa*. Marx defined an individual's class by their relationship to the mode of production. Capitalists owned the means of production, whereas the working class had only labour power. For Marx, society was being torn apart by two hostile camps, two great classes: the bourgeoisie (those with property) and the proletariat (those without). After decades of being largely ignored, Marx's idea of class has returned in the twenty-first century as an analytical tool, an explanatory concept, and a vital axis of political mobilisation to better understand systems of economic inequality. Class is once again a legitimate method of challenging the practices of global neoliberal austerity, with several scholars demonstrating a refreshed interest in class identity, class exploitation, and class conflict. Marx's approach to class continues to be influential in this regard.

9

NATURE

The major challenge facing our time is dealing with the consequences of human-made environmental destruction. Carbon emissions, chemical pollution, deforestation, and rising global temperatures all threaten our future. But humanity faces not just warmer weather, but a crisis of the Earth system. In 2002, the Nobel prize-winning scientist Paul Crutzen coined the term 'the Anthropocene', arguing that human-induced changes in the Earth system were of such deep impact that we could now speak of a new epoch in the Earth's history (Crutzen, 2002). It is a sobering thought that the next few decades will determine whether humans will be able to continue to survive on Earth.

This chapter will show how Marx is a philosopher who has long been concerned with nature and the natural world. It will introduce a range of approaches to Marxist ecology, which, beginning with the work of Marx himself, explores the critical relations between capitalism and environmental crisis. Marxist ecology is bound up with other approaches, blending 'green' economics, eco-socialism, and anti-capitalism. Most powerfully, Marxist ecology argues that the expansion of the capitalist system is the primary cause of planetary ecological crisis, and that new models of social and economic existence are required to avert irreparable environmental destruction. I will introduce Marx's largely overlooked writings on ecology along-side pioneering readings by John Bellamy Foster (1953–), Paul Burkett (1956–), and Kohei Saito (1987–). As will become clear, for Marx, we do not live outside or beyond nature, but inescapably within it.

Historically, Marx has not been considered an ecological thinker. His insights on class structures and industrial production did not immediately lend themselves to the environmental movement. For John P. Clark, Marx is more concerned with production than its ecological cost:

> Marx's Promethean and Oedipal 'man' is a being who is not at home in nature, who does not see the earth as the 'household' of ecology. Rather, he is an indomitable spirit who must subjugate nature in his quest for self-realization [...] For such a being, the forces of nature, whether in the form of his own unmastered internal nature or the menacing powers of external nature, must be subdued.
>
> (Clark, 1989)

In Greek myth, Prometheus stole fire from the gods and created humanity. The story glorifies human conquest over nature, treating it as an instrument of change. The charge of a 'Promethean' vision, in which capitalist development of the productive forces allows humans to overcome natural constraints, is a common criticism of Marx's critique of capital. Many ecologists have dismissed Marx's writings on the basis that his insights are potentially destructive towards nature. Criticisms even come from those conversant with Marx's writings. As Michael Löwy argues, while Marx makes some references in *Capital* to the exhaustion of nature by capital, 'Marx does not possess an integrated ecological perspective' (Löwy, 1997, cited in Burkett, 2014, 34). For Löwy:

> There is a tendency in Marx (pronounced in the Marxism after Marx) to consider the development of the forces of production as the principal vector of progress, to adopt an unfairly uncritical attitude toward industrial civilization, particularly its destructive relationship to nature.
>
> (*ibid.*, 34)

But for ecological Marxists, Marx's approach to nature and the natural world possesses 'an inner logic, coherence, and analytical power' that often goes unrecognised (*ibid.*, xxix). In the following section we will see how.

MARX AND THE ENDS OF THE EARTH

Marx turned to ecology in the 1860s. As with other aspects of his writings, there is no single critique of the environment and ecology: these ideas are present throughout Marx's journalism, scientific notebooks, and *Capital*. The fact that Marx did not write a sustained polemic on ecology does not mean that he didn't articulate an ecological vision.

Marx's writings on ecology discuss capitalist agriculture, climate, soil, botany, land rent, social relations in the countryside, philosophical naturalism, and evolutionary theory. His personal library shows an extensive collection of books on these matters, suggesting he took seriously the relationships among capital, humans, and nature. His first foray into these areas was a defence of the rights of peasants to collect wood from the forest, when he was editor of the *Rheinische Zeitung*. I discussed this in Chapter One but, when thinking about Marx as a philosopher of nature, it is clear that it was an ecological critique of the expropriation of nature that led him to turn to political economy. Marx clearly approached this issue from an ecological standpoint: in picking up wood, peasants once had access to the commons (the resources accessible to all members of society). But the natural riches of the world – wood, water, and farmland – were being claimed as private property for individual profit. For Marx, ecology and economy are closely connected.

The plunder of the natural world was attacked more forcefully in *Capital*, which revealed capitalism's destructive relation to the ecological realm through the theft of what Marx called the 'elemental powers of nature' (*MECW1*, 234). In chapter 27 of *Capital*, Marx talks about the ways in which peasants had 'enjoyed the right to exploit the common land which gave them pasture to their cattle, and furnished them with timber, fire-wood' and space for growing their crops (Marx, 1990, 877). Marx describes a 'systematic theft of communal property' from the fifteenth century onward, in which capitalists enacted a 'forcible expropriation of the people' from the land which once belonged to them (*ibid.*, 881). In the course of capitalist development, by the 'nineteenth century the very memory of the connection between agricultural labourer and communal property had, of course, vanished' (*ibid.*, 889). This process forced peasants, who were used to working on the land, into factory labour. Capitalists had 'conquered the field for capitalist agriculture', Marx writes, 'incorporated the [free] soil into capital, and created for the urban industries the necessary supplies of free and rightless proletarians' (*ibid.*, 895). As Marx makes clear, peasants' livelihoods were destroyed to create a cheap and dispensable class of industrial workers.

MARX'S ECOLOGY

John Bellamy Foster's *Marx's Ecology: Materialism and Nature* (2000) is one of the most important contributions to this debate. Foster argues that while Marx has 'often been characterised as an anti-ecological thinker', he was in fact deeply concerned with the ever-changing relationships between humans and the natural world (Foster, 2000, 1). He argues 'Marx's world view was deeply, and indeed systematically, ecological [...] and his ecological perspective derived from his materialism' (*ibid.*). Such a position, when first articulated, ran contrary to all other interpretations of Marx. 'My path to ecological Marxism' writes Foster, 'was blocked by the Marxism that I had learned over the years' (*ibid.*). The theoretical legacy of other Marxist thinkers, such as Georg Lukács (1885–1971) and Antonio Gramsci (1891–1937), often denied the importance of connecting Marxism to the 'wider natural-physical realm' by focusing on other aspects of interest such as reification or hegemony. In coming to think seriously about Marx as an ecological thinker, writes Foster, 'What I discovered, much to my astonishment, was a story that had something of the character of a literary detective story, in which various disparate clues led inexorably to a single, surprising source' (*ibid.*). For Marxist ecologists, reading Marx in the twenty-first century necessitates a critical orientation: we can now see him as a philosopher who 'develops a revolutionary ecological view of great importance to us today' (*ibid.*, 2). You can neither understand nor practice ecology today without coming to terms – whatever those terms may be – with Marx's writings on capitalism. For Foster, Marx's ecology can best be understood by turning to another great thinker of the nineteenth century: Charles Darwin. Darwin's ideas immediately attracted the interest of Marx, who was trying to bring a revolution to society with his own work.

MARX AND DARWIN

When Darwin published *On the Origin of Species* (1859), Marx and Engels read it eagerly. That Darwin held political views far from their own did not bother them. While they held certain disagreements about the book, both men praised Darwin's efforts: Marx stated that it contains 'in the field of natural history, [...] the basis for our views' (*MECW41*, 232). Marx and Engels often incorporated the latest findings of science into their work, but they did not need to wait for Darwin's insights on evolution to propose a science of society. The evolution of animal species was an idea in circulation before Darwin, and was already part of their shared interests before 1859. In an 1857 draft introduction to *A Contribution to the Critique of Political Economy*, Marx uses an evolutionary analogy to understand the connection between bourgeois economy as the highest phase of development, and 'the vanished social formations' of past societies, just as 'Human anatomy contains a key to the anatomy of the ape (Marx, 1993, 105). Marx did, however, read and re-read Darwin's book, seeking some natural-scientific basis for his own critique of political economy. He makes two references to Darwin in *Capital*, in two footnotes, which he hurriedly added before the book went to press. They were positive remarks, with Marx calling Darwin's book an 'epoch making work' (Marx, 1990, 461).

Marx admired Darwin so much that he sent him a copy of *Capital*. Darwin delayed his return letter by some months, but thanked Marx for the honour of receiving the book and wished he were 'more worthy to receive it, by understanding more of the deep & important subject of political economy' (Darwin,

Correspondence Project, 2020). It is likely that Darwin did not read more than a couple pages of *Capital*. By this point, Darwin had retired from public life to his country house in Kent and spent his days on botany. While Marx could appreciate the importance of Darwin's work, the latter chose not to pursue the significance of Marx.

But Marx regarded his work and Darwinism as separate but parallel theories, one on natural history, and the other on human history. In the *Economic and Philosophical Manuscripts*, Marx had already discovered that productive activity is the basis of human history. 'Industry', writes Marx, 'is the actual, historical relationship of nature, and therefore of natural science, to man' (*MECW3*, 303). A more detailed exploration of the relationship between humans and the lived environment is offered in the *Grundrisse*, where Marx writes on the rift created between nature and capitalist society.

> It is not the unity of living and active humanity with the natural, inorganic conditions of their metabolic exchange with nature, and hence their appropriation of nature, which requires explanation as a result of a historic process, but rather the separation between these inorganic conditions of human existence and this active existence, a separation which is completely posited only in the relation of wage labour and capital.
>
> (Marx, 1993, 489)

Where most of us would begin by thinking about nature as external to us, as a resource for humans to use, Marx provides a critique of the alienated nature of bourgeoise society. We are separate from nature, argues Marx, because capitalism treats nature as separate from us. Capitalism is a mode of social and economic organisation that allows for a competitive, profit-driven development of nature, placing greater and greater pressure on the global biosphere.

In the *Economic and Philosophical Manuscripts*, Marx analysed alienation from nature in an ecologically sensitive manner. While these documents are best known for the development of the concept of the alienation of labour, Marx shows how this alienation is inseparable from the natural world. He explained that 'Man lives from nature, i.e. nature is his body, and he must maintain a continuing dialogue with it if he is not too die. To say that man's physical and mental life is linked to nature simply means that nature is linked to itself, for man is a part of nature' (Marx, 1992, 328). In the same work, Marx developed a radical critique of the pollution of large towns. For workers in the towns, this freedom meant a 'freedom' from what had been considered basic human needs. As Marx put it, in such large towns: 'Even the need for fresh air ceases to be a need for the worker. Man reverts once more to living in a cave, but the cave is now polluted by the mephitic and pestilential breath of civilization' (*ibid.*, 359–60) For Marx, the needs of men and women living in towns and cities, and working in factories, were not being met in ways that allowed them to reach their potential. From this point onwards, Marx would routinely relate humans to nature. In Volume 3 of *Capital*, he embarks on an ecologically informed analysis that builds a complex picture of the plight of the working class in relation to the inhumanity of capitalists and factory owners. Marx considers 'The Genesis of Capitalist Ground Rent', focusing on the capitalist exploitation of the worker, land, and soil:

> Large landed property reduces the agricultural population to an ever decreasing minimum and confronts it with an ever growing industrial population crammed together in large towns; in this way it produces conditions that provoke an irreparable rift in the interdependent process of social metabolism, a metabolism prescribed by the natural laws of life itself. The result of this is a squandering of the vitality of the soil [...] the industrial system applied to agriculture also enervates the workers there, while industry and trade for their part provide agriculture with the means of exhausting the soil.
>
> (Marx, 1991, 949)

Marx would make a similar point in Volume 1, in a section on 'Large-Scale Industry and Agriculture'. Marx writes that capitalist production disturbs the 'interaction between man and the earth [...] progress in capitalist agriculture is a progress in the art, not only of robbing the worker, but of robbing the soil [...] capitalist production, therefore, only develops the technique of and the degree of combination of the social process of production by simultaneously undermining the original sources of wealth – the soil and the worker' (Marx, 1990, 637–38). As capitalism extends its reach across the globe, the soil itself becomes a marketable commodity, one to be exploited, just like the worker.

Kohei Saito examines Marx's natural-scientific notebooks. Importantly, these nature notebooks have only recently been discovered. Given this, it is impossible, argues Saito, 'to comprehend the full scope of Marx's critique of political economy if one ignores the ecological dimension' (Saito, 2017). Marx, then, cared deeply about the changing human relationship to nature. If Marx's critique of the capitalist mode of production sought to build a radically egalitarian society, then he also wanted to construct a sustainable eco-socialist world.

Engels had, in surveying the conditions of the working class in Manchester, mounted his own ecological critique. Using first-hand observation and the reports of physicians and factory inspectors, Engels presented a vivid picture of the poor state of public health. He described filthy streets, homes, and courtyards, overcrowding, bad sanitation, and poor lighting and ventilation. Workers had extreme dietary deficiencies, and routinely suffered mental and physical illnesses. Infectious diseases, such as typhus and tuberculosis, were spread by severe air and water pollution. By the time of their joint composition of *The German Ideology*, Marx and Engels give us a rare vision of a post-capitalist world in which humans are free from the drudgery of work and able to pursue conscious and creative activity in any branch they wish. This activity may involve rearing cattle in the morning, fishing in the afternoon, and criticising after dinner. This problematic pastoral vision of the future is under threat. As Gregory Claeys remarks, 'if we continue to fail to act on the climate crisis, then there will be nothing to fish or hunt, but plenty to criticise' (Claeys, 2018, 461).

SUMMARY

The intensity of environmental devastation has shifted the focus of Marxism's critical gaze. Traditional Marxism was more concerned with the structural conflict between workers and the owners of the means of production, a situation in which the capitalist class enrich themselves through the surplus value created by the proletariat. Marx, however, is not simply a philosopher of industrial capitalism. He is a thinker deeply attuned to the importance of the environment, ecology, and the natural world. It has only been possible to grasp Marx's engagement with environmental matters with the recent (and continued) translation of a range of newly discovered natural scientific notebooks. In these notebooks, Marx provides an ecological critique of capitalism. Whether Marx made a series of stunning revelations about ecology, or whether Marx provides a complete and systematic engagement developed in parallel with his critique of political economy, is a subject of dispute among scholars. Capitalism has generated environmental disaster and ecological destruction. Given the profound and urgent nature of this realisation, scholars across different disciplines have turned to the study of nature, world ecology, and the environment. Despite being a nineteenth-century thinker, Marx's insights on ecology and the natural world remain of great importance. This may initially appear surprising, as it is often assumed that Marx cared more about industrial development and the growth of productive forces than the changing human relationship to nature. Fundamentally, as Marx makes clear, the ecological crisis has its causes in the capitalist-generated exploitation of people and planet. The rediscovery of Marx's ecology is of immense importance to the development of new forms of struggle against global capitalism. We can only hope that these green shoots grow quickly.

10

COMMUNISM

In Wolfgang Becker's film *Goodbye Lenin!* (2003), an East Berlin woman, Christine, suffers amnesia at the precise moment of the fall of the Berlin Wall. Fearing for her fragile state, her son Alex stage-manages a transfigured version of the past. He fakes newsreels and searches out foodstuffs no longer available in post-Wall food chains. In effect, Alex creates a new reality: a disjunction between Christine's experience of the world around her and the post-Wall situation. This world is torn apart when Christine wakes up and walks out onto the street. In the ending of the film, a dazed and confused Christine speaks to a young man from Western Germany, puzzles over an Ikea sign, and watches a huge airborne statue of Lenin go past her. As the statue swings through the city, it momentarily aligns with Christine's position, the outstretched arm of Lenin beckoning towards her. This image is comic but conceals layers of depth. The gesture is not hostile, but framed as kindly, welcoming; an invitation to Christine to remember the emancipatory potential of communism, distorted though it was under the German Democratic Republic. As Roger Hillman argues, this is 'history in the subjunctive' or 'socialism in surreal mode' (Hillman, 2006, 224). In focusing on the interim between the dismantling of the GDR and the reconstruction of German national identity, the film presents a past that never was, 'flashbacks to a non-existent world' (*ibid.*,

224). In approaching history in the subjunctive mood, the film is less about the recreation of an illusion than about socialism as it should have been.

Becker's film is utopian, exploring creative dimensions beyond written history. For communism began as a dream and ended as a nightmare. In the communist regimes of the twentieth century, millions suffered physical and psychological horrors in what was meant to be the creation of an exploitation-free post-capitalist society. All of these systems ended in failure, with many societies changing so dramatically that the original idea of a better world for all was quickly lost. Two points of clarification are necessary. First, most communist states, such as China, adopt capitalist principles. Second, communism as an idea is immensely diverse. Many have contributed views, but there are also many interesting 'gaps, ambiguities, and contradictions within the works of some of the best-known theorists', particularly Marx himself (Holmes, 2009, 1). Nevertheless, at its core, communism is a theory of an exploitation-free future where classes are absent, property is owned by the community, and work is based on a principle of contribution rather than survival. Some of the so-called communist countries have failed to meet even these criteria, showing a distinction between the theory of communism and the practice of states claiming to be building it.

In this chapter I will introduce Marx's ideas on communism, which are quite different to the communist societies of the previous century. I discussed the *Communist Manifesto* in Chapter Three, and while this is an immensely important document, containing most of Marx's key ideas on capitalism, communism, and revolution, it does not contain *all* of Marx's thoughts on communism as a social, political, and economic ideology. Like any other thinker, his ideas changed over the course of his life. Firstly, however, I will begin by introducing some of the former and still existing communist states so we can better understand Marx's distinctive contribution.

COMMUNISM NOW

The collapse of communism was one of the defining events of the last century. By the 1990s, only five of more than twenty communist states had survived. China, Vietnam, and Laos had introduced such radical market-oriented measures that their designation as 'communist' was increasingly under doubt (Holmes, 2009, 118). North Korea was engaged in a nightmare of famine, isolation, repression, and mass delusion, while the triumph of the Castro revolution, with impressive advances in healthcare and education, had led to an economic downturn. The collapse of the soviet-dominated bloc in Eastern Europe, then the USSR, put an end to twentieth-century communism. In November 1989, the Berlin Wall – a large guarded concrete barrier that divided the communist East of the city from the democratic West – was pulled down, ushering in German reunification and the end of the Cold War.

The events surrounding the fall of communism have inspired numerous novels. John le Carré's (1931–) spy thriller *The Spy Who Came in From the Cold* (1963) follows Alec Leamas, a British agent who is sent to East Germany. The novel opens with a nail-biting scene: the defection of an East Berlin double agent, who tries to make it across the Wall to the West. Le Carré's novel dramatises the ideological conflicts of the twentieth century – between East and West, communism, and capitalism – in the struggle to create a worldwide political transformation. At its peak, more than a third of the world's population lived under regimes of communist power. These regimes have claimed a commitment to Marxism, but, as I will now show, there is little connection between these societies and Marx's ideas on a post-capitalist future.

THE COLD WAR

The Cold War was a period of profound geopolitical tension between the Soviet Union and the United States, lasting from the end of the Second World War to the dissolution of the Soviet Union in 1991. The term 'cold' captures the lack of large-scale military combat between the two superpowers, although both supported small-scale regional conflicts known as proxy wars. The powerful nuclear arsenals held by the two countries discouraged any pre-emptive attacks, a situation referred to as mutually assured destruction (MAD). The Cold War has left a significant legacy, placing into the public domain themes of intelligence-gathering, surveillance, and espionage. Tensions among the United States, Europe, and Russia have continued in the twenty-first century, which some historians and cultural commentators have referred to as a new or second Cold War.

MARX'S COMMUNISM

Marx is the most important figure in communism, and his contributions provided a broad theoretical framework for future thinkers. Marx's ideas on communism were sceptical of idealist sentiments (truth, morality, justice), and he preferred to establish his arguments about the necessity of change on an exhaustive study of capitalism. He considered it essential to rest communism upon a rigorous scientific foundation. His analysis in *Capital* was the cornerstone of this. While others made passionate public appeals, Marx's ideas were backed up by theoretical insights.

Marx's earliest writings on communism are all from the 1840s: including the *Economic and Philosophical Manuscripts*, *The German Ideology*, and the *Communist Manifesto*. I have already discussed these works in previous chapters, and I will now turn to focus on Marx's later writings. By the time of *Capital*, and his involvement with the International Workingmen's Association in London, Marx's views on communism and revolution had undergone a process of development and clarification. He remained a revolutionary and a communist, but he now had a different understanding of what these two meant. Towards the end of his life, Marx was more receptive to trade unions, cooperatives, and political reform movements. He was optimistic about deploying political struggle to enrich and develop existing democratic institutions. He also arrived at a different position on revolution which he considered to be a transitional process rather than an event. As Gareth Stedman Jones argues, this sense of optimism was shattered after Marx's death, in which the creation of communism was thought to be the result of the collapse of capitalism rather than the activity of progressive political parties (Stedman Jones, 2017, 187). This was the context in which Marxism developed. For Stedman Jones, twentieth-century revolutionaries largely obscured Marx's position of revolution as a process, creating a connection between Marx and the newly formed 'Marxist' language of violent overthrow. Party leaders like Lenin (1870–1924) based their political strategies on what they conceived to be a correct reading of a small number of Marxist texts, all of which were taken from the years before the publication of *Capital* and Marx's involvement with the International. In later life, Marx broadened his idea of revolution to encompass 'the political ratification of changes which had already occurred or were already occurring in civil society. The greater the extent of such changes the greater the possibility of imagining a revolution that did not need to be violent' (Stedman Jones, 2017, 118).

In Marx's final years, communism was considered to be cooperation combined with communal government. *The Critique of the Gotha Programme* (1875), one of the last texts Marx wrote, offers the clearest indication of Marx's idea of communism coming through different stages. The first stage of a communist society would include equal rights, pay, and reciprocity, with Marx writing that 'the same amount of labour which he has given society in one form he receives back in another' (Marx, 2019, 1030). In a more advanced phase of communist society, when 'the springs of cooperative wealth flow more abundantly', then 'can society wholly cross the narrow horizon of bourgeois right and inscribe on its banner: "From each according to his abilities, to each according to his needs!"' (*ibid.*, 1031). Under this more developed form of communism, rewards based on labour are no longer necessary, with access to goods and resources based on requirement. While the philosophical premises of this are attractive, in their focus on free activity, cooperation, and need over luxury, many questions are left unresolved.

Annoyingly, Marx never wrote a complete, detailed study of communism. The *Manifesto* is not it, but is rather a *tour de force* document aimed at showcasing a small number of key ideas and stamping communism on the political horizon. Marx was encouraged to write a book on communism by Engels, who in

1851 asked Marx to explain 'the much-coveted secret [...] the much vaunted "positive" being what you "really" want (Engels, *MECW38*, 493). Marx, however, maintained that communists are not utopians and therefore had no plan for the exact layout of a future society. His remarks on communist societies are scattered across his works but, most powerfully, Marx saw communism as the beginning of history, describing our time under capitalism as prehistory. Typically, communism is misrepresented as a finished or final situation in which the societies achieve freedom from capitalism. But for Marx, history, real history, had not yet begun. Only when individuals were free from the compulsions of the capitalist marketplace, and able to pursue conscious and creative activity, would history have started.

Marx, then, produced puzzling, cryptic, even contradictory images of what future communist societies might look like. Most of Marx's views on how this would occur in practice are, at best, problematic. Quite often, however, he wished to confine himself to a critical analysis of the facts rather than provide what he called 'recipes for the cook-shops of the future' (Marx, 1990, 99). Marx was hesitant of providing detailed instructions of how future communist societies would operate. In *The German Ideology*, Marx argued that communism was not a set of prescriptions but a political movement that could not be anticipated in advance. 'Communism is for us not a *state of affairs* that is to be established, an ideal to which reality [will] have to adjust itself', Marx wrote, but 'the *real* movement that abolishes the present state of things' (Marx, CW5, 49). A communism based on claims of peace and justice would be at odds with Marx's searching examination of the antagonistic nature of capitalist social relations. But Marx undoubtedly had ideals to realise, such as cooperation, self-actualisation, and the society of free producers (communal ownership of the means of production).

MARX AND REVOLUTION

Marx was vague about what would follow a successful revolution. He proposed that a new kind of society would emerge – communism – in which the ruling class had been abolished. There would be no alienation in a communist society, the state would wither away, and individuals would be free from the tyranny of work. If this is the end point, Marx is also unclear about the exact transition from capitalism to communism, which involves a series of steps including proletarian revolution, economic crisis, the political party, and critique. Marx's views on communism are illuminating and opaque in equal measure.

But Marx was clear that a communist revolution could occur only in advanced industrial societies; rural, agricultural societies would not be ready for such large-scale changes, as they did not possess an industrial working class. For Marx, the driving force of history was class relationships, meaning that the escalating tensions between the two major classes (bourgeoise and proletariat) build up over time and result in revolution. Whether or not less economically developed societies would need to undergo capitalist development was an important question, and one Marx turned to in the final decade of his life. He considered Russian economic development, began learning the language, and corresponded with Russian thinkers. Marx was preoccupied with a new question: could communism be achieved without capitalism?

The Bolsheviks, a political party led by Lenin, thought that communism could only occur in a developed industrial society. A member of the Bolsheviks, Alexander Bogdanov (1873–1928), wrote a science-fiction novel, *Red Star: The First Bolshevik Utopia* (1908), which imagines communism on Mars. In the novel, a Russian scientist named Leonid is whisked away by a Martian called Menni, to learn about the successful creation of a technological advanced society that had achieved freedom and happiness. As a Bolshevik, Bogdanov modelled the society of Mars after his own ideal. 'Blood is being shed for the sake of a better future', says one Martian to Leonid. 'But in order to wage the struggle, we must know the future' (Bogdanov *et al.*, 1984, 1). As the subtitle indicates, the novel is an experiment in utopia: through a radical juxtaposition of the two worlds, it asks readers to imagine constructing a successful communist society through the use of science and technology.

THE RUSSIAN REVOLUTION (1917–1923)

The Russian Revolution began at the end of the First World War. In February 1917, a longstanding discontent with the Russian monarchy erupted into mass protests against food rationing. The Russian Tsar, Nicholas II, abdicated, bringing an end to dynastic rule. A temporary government – called the Provisional Government – was established to carry out all the major reforms. A second Revolution in October was led by the Bolshevik Party, under Lenin, who mobilised workers, and militias to overthrow the Provisional Government and transfer all power to the party. After a bitter Civil War between the Bolsheviks (Reds) and counter-revolutionary forces (Whites), Russia was renamed the Union of Soviet Socialist Republics (USSR).

Marx's *Capital* had been translated into Russian and had sold well. But Russia was an immense land mass dominated by peasants, arable farming, and communes. It posed obvious challenges to Marx's comments that 'social revolution was only possible […] where alongside capitalist production the industrial proletariat accounts for at least a significant portion of the people' (Marx, *MECW24*, 518). This question forced Marx to return to his argument that industrial capitalism would precede socialism. For Gregory Claeys, 'this engagement represented a fundamental challenge to the *Manifesto*'s model of communism emerging only when the highest stage of capitalist development had sown the seeds of its own downfall' (Claeys, 2018, 205). Marx speculated on the possibility of revolution in Russia, and later wrote that the historical inevitability of the expropriation of agricultural producers was 'expressly limited to the countries of western Europe' (Marx, *MECW46*, 71–72). Marx always made an effort to incorporate the latest research into his thinking. His analysis of the possibility of revolution in non-capitalist countries, while partial and incomplete, show his ability to re-examine key ideas in relation to changing historical circumstances.

THE DICTATORSHIP OF THE PROLETARIAT

Following a successful revolution in a capitalist country, and before the final stage of communism could be reached, there would occur a temporary or transitional stage: 'the dictatorship of the proletariat'. This term or its equivalent was used three times by Marx, and first occurred in a series of articles later titled *The Class Struggles in France 1848–1850*. The *Gotha Programme* makes a reference to a 'corresponding period of transition in the political sphere and in this period the state can only take the form of a revolutionary dictatorship of the proletariat' (Marx, 2019, 1039). Marx never defines this stage properly, other than as an intermediary in the transition from capitalism to communism. However, Marx's comments must be understood in relation to his life-long commitment to democracy.

In the *Manifesto*, Marx writes that it is essential to 'raise the proletariat to the position of the ruling class to win the battle of democracy', and both he and Engels supported democratic parties and movements (Marx and Engels, 1998, 12). Marx's theories on the revolutionary proletariat and economic crisis were not simply theoretical, however, as he continually sought to locate real examples by which to realise his theory in practice.

Marx was especially impressed by the Paris Commune, a series of revolutionary events in Paris, that occurred in spring 1871. The outbreak of social revolution came at a fortuitous time and spoke directly to Marx's studies on the practical transition from capitalism to communism. 'The great social measure of the Commune', wrote Marx, 'was its own working existence, rather than any ideals it sought to realise' (Marx, 2019, 901). Marx knew the Commune was a place of improvised political inventions. With its founding, alternative structures of governance quickly emerged. For instance, the Women's Union for the Defence of Paris made substantial contributions in the form of staffing ambulances, filling sandbags, and even fighting on the barricades. The Union addressed gender inequalities by providing pay for women and organising production through cooperation in local workshops (Ross, 2015, 12). Such actions offer glimpses of a possible and desirable future; a future that had not been written in advance, but that emerged through a collective effort.

THE PARIS COMMUNE

The Paris Commune was a worker-led insurrection that occupied the centre of the French capital for some 70 days in 1871. Workers implemented a new radical socialist and revolutionary government that transformed the city into an autonomous commune and recalibrated social life according to principles of freedom, cooperation, and association. The government was supported by anarchist and communist refugees and exiles including Marx, Peter Kropotkin (1842–1921), and William Morris (1834–1896), for whom the existence of the Commune represented a turning point in their political philosophies. The ambitions and accomplishments of the Commune were met with intense violence and the workers were eventually suppressed by the French army in May. As the historian Eric Hobsbawm notes, the commune provoked an 'international outburst of hysteria among the rulers of Europe and among its terrified middle classes' (Hobsbawm, 1995, 84). Despite its eventual defeat, the commune became a symbol for emerging socialist movements in Europe and abroad, and is still a symbol of radical hope today.

Marx's analysis of the struggle of the Communards (members of the Commune) was given in *The Civil War in France*. This pamphlet was written on behalf of the General Council of the International, while Marx was living in London. The Commune had the support of European working classes, and meetings and demonstrations were held in solidarity in England and elsewhere. The text was approved by the General Council in May, only a few days after the defeat of the Commune, and rushed to the printers. *The Civil War in France* remains one of the most important texts of Marx's later years (along with *The Critique of the Gotha Programme*), and the most widely circulated of Marx's texts written during his own time. It gives a forceful reading of the measures undertaken by the Commune, why it was an important revolutionary model, and an examination of the key theoretical questions it raised.

Marx had initially opposed the Commune because he believed that revolution had to be international. Additionally, he opposed violence, preferring protest, political organisation, and the education of workers. But once the Commune existed, he became a strong supporter and reformulated his understanding of revolution in response to these events. But while the Commune put together the elements of a new political imaginary, its members were crushed. The brutal response of the French Government fractured radical politics for some time afterward. The Commune is remembered for its radical potential and for inspiring the socialist revolutions of the twentieth century.

MARX, COMMUNISM, AND UTOPIA

This final section examines the relationship between Marx's communism and utopia. Marx was writing during the time of the utopian socialists, a group of radicals and philanthropists including Robert Owen (1771–1858), Charles Fourier (1772–1837), and Henri de Saint-Simon (1760–1825). Proclaiming 'Liberty, Equality, Fraternity', the Utopian Socialists were concerned with creating practical experiments to reveal how utopia might work. Owen founded a commune where workers and their children were given free education. Similar experiments were conducted in the United States, while other progressives attacked the institution of marriage, which gave little liberty to women. All these experiments were short-lived, but they nevertheless demonstrated the possibility of progress by enacting programmes of social and political change.

UTOPIA

Many scholars, popular usages, and dictionaries think of utopias as ideal but impractical societies. Such pronouncements misunderstand Marx's relation to utopia, and show a remarkably limited understanding of utopia as a literary and philosophical category. Utopia is far less a totalising vision of perfection than a speculative discourse on the not-yet-achieved; a society that is not perfect, but better than the original. The term 'utopia' cannot be reduced to the history of the word coined by Sir Thomas More in 1516. However, More's *Utopia* remains a useful conceptual starting point. More's book was written in response to the foreclosing of common land, growing inequality, and capital punishment. It described a remote island where property was held in common, and where 'though no man has anything, yet all are rich'. Though full of radical ideas, *Utopia* was not a blueprint for a future society, but rather aimed at revealing the gross inequalities of the time. Similar works following More's included Tommaso Campanella's *The City of the Sun* (1602), Francis Bacon's *New Atlantis* (1627), and James Harrington's *The Commonwealth of Oceana* (1657).

Marx was positive about the utopian socialists. In 1875, he praised their work, claiming that 'German theoretical Socialism will never forget that it stands on the shoulders of Saint-Simon, Fourier, Owen, three men who despite their fantasies and utopianism are to be reckoned among the most significant minds of all times' (*Selected Correspondence*, 1970, 250). Utopian socialism had 'anticipated with genius countless matters' but it was now necessary to break from these 'fantastic anticipations' for the objectivity of 'scientific insight' (*ibid.*, 250). Marx did not object to utopia *per se*, but rather was critical of speculative solutions to practical problems. In a letter written before his death, Marx expressed a stronger opposition to utopia, arguing these 'fantastic anticipations of the programme of action for a revolution of the future only divert us from the struggle of the present' (Marx, CW46, 67). For Marx, communism could not be achieved by constructing fantastical islands in the sea of capital, but required a total transformation of society.

CONCLUSION

The century-long epic of communism contains numerous false starts, abrupt endings, and unexpected revivals. The Cuban, Chinese, and Soviet traditions display little that is attractive for emancipatory politics. The crash of 2008 put a large dent in the neoliberal consensus and ushered in populist movements on both left and right. In the UK, the socialist Jeremy Corbyn was crushed in the 2019 General Election, while in the USA, Bernie Sanders has twice failed to secure the Democratic nomination. But most citizens are dissatisfied with capitalism, austerity, social inequality, ecological crisis, and political corruption and there is a dawning recognition that a new kind of economy is needed: fairer, more inclusive, less exploitative, and less destructive of society and the planet. But communism, a system still tied to the tyrannies of Lenin, Stalin, and the Russian Gulags, is not at all appealing. Marx, however, inspired efforts to end imperialism, colonialism, and the oppression of workers. In challenging exploitative systems, Marx will always have a place. We may arrive at a place much like Marx imagined, but it will be through democracy and progressive modes of political interaction, rather than revolution.

But communism continues to pose powerful challenges to capitalism. In 2009, the Birkbeck Institute for the Humanities hosted 'The Idea of Communism' conference, an event that attracted a large audience and a host of radical intellectuals including Alain Badiou (1937–), Jodi Dean (1962–), and Slavoj Žižek (1949–). The conference was repeated in Paris, Berlin, New York, and Seoul, and copies of the speakers' talks appear in three edited collections (Douzinas and Žižek, 2010; Žižek, 2013; Žižek and Taek-Gwang Lee, 2016). The radical publishing house Verso launched a series of books connected to these events, which examined communism as a philosophical and political idea. Bhaskar Sunkara's *The Socialist Manifesto* (2019) argued that current class inequalities called for more radial forms of wealth distribution; while Kristen Ghodsee's *Why Women Have Better Sex Under Socialism* (2018) argued that socialism was more conducive to economic independence, gender equality, and sexual freedom. Aaron Bastani, in *Fully Automated Luxury Communism* (2019), argues that new technologies of automation will liberate humanity from work and create communal luxury; while Jodi Dean's *Comrade* (2019) calls for a return to a term that indexes a political relation, a set of expectations, and a common goal of radical action.

SUMMARY

Marx is the most important intellectual figure in communism. He never wrote a book-length study of communism, or demarcated what a communist society would look like. His often puzzling and cryptic ideas about communism are scattered throughout his writings. Marx's ideas underwent a process of refinement and clarification throughout his life, meaning that the type of communism he proposed as a young man is different from the one he championed in later years. Despite this, Marx was always attached to ideas of radical justice, egalitarianism, and freedom, what he called 'the development of the richness of human nature as an end in itself' (Marx, 1993, 708). Marx's ideas on the transition from capitalism to communism are complex and are not complete.

AFTER MARX

Marx was a restless, creative thinker, whose works exploded in different directions. He did not have the time, the will, or the peace required to straighten them all out. For all their genius, Marx's works are untidy and occasionally unclear. His use of dialectics suggests that none of them are complete, but this is a virtue rather than a hindrance. As Samir Amin argues, we must

> continue the work that Marx merely began, even though that beginning was of an unequaled power. It is not to stop at Marx, but to start from him [...] Marx is *boundless*, because the radical critique that he initiated is itself boundless, always incomplete, and must always be the object of its own critique.
>
> (Amin, 2010, 9–10)

Marx's ideas had, and continue to have, a major impact across the Humanities. The challenges he set out have influenced all the major critical approaches, including structuralism, post-structuralism, feminism, postcolonialism, critical race studies, deconstruction, historicism, Marxism, and post-Marxism. Marx's wide-ranging interest in literature and culture, along with his theorisations of their political and philosophical import-ance, is of immense importance to those in English studies. Crucially, Marx provided no complete or systematic theory of aesthetic criticism, but his ideas lay down challenges that future generations could not ignore.

Marx is the greatest analyst of capitalism. He spent his entire life criticising the operations that sustained it, the concepts that enabled it, and the theories that supported it. In his three-volume master work, *Capital*, he rigorously pointed out the conditions of inequality, exploitation, and oppression that capitalism creates and relies on. But his ideas have also became a material force, influencing social democracy, communism, anticolonial movements, and anticapitalist protests.

Without Marx we would still have revolution, capitalism, and communism, He did not invent any of these terms, but he did place a distinctive stamp upon them, to the point that any serious consideration of them must mention Marx in the same breadth. Marx's own formulations, including his focus on class, class struggle, the dictatorship of the proletariat, labour, alienation, value, ideology, false consciousness, capital, the commodity, the fetishism of commodities, his idea of the 'mode of production', and the method of analysis Engels called 'historical materialism' or 'the materialist conception of history', all point to an intellectual figure of striking originality. Without his focus on economic matters and material circumstances, we would know a great deal less about capitalism. Without his idea of the base and superstructure, we would be discussing literature and culture in far less critical modes. Marx achieved all this by continually confronting the realities of historical oppression under capitalism and the repressed potentiality of human society.

Marx's politics did not survive the next century. The Marx constructed in the twentieth century 'bore only an incidental resemblance' to the nineteenth-century critic of capitalism (Stedman Jones, 2017, 595). Political parties obscured Marx's position on revolution, with leaders conducting strategies based upon what they conceived to be a correct reading of a small number of 'Marxist' texts, all of which were taken from the years before *Capital* and Marx's involvement with the International Workingmen's Association (*ibid.*, 118). Marx, it is clear, become more democratic in later life and treated revolution as a process, not an event: 'Successful revolution meant the political ratification of changes which had already occurred or were already occurring in civil society. The greater the extent of such changes, the greater the possibility of imagining a revolution that did not need to be violent' (*ibid.*, 118). But even in the *Manifesto*, Marx made clear he supported trade unions, socialist parties, and working-class organisations, which all sought democratic gains. After Marx's death in 1883, few could have anticipated the trajectory of Marx's ideas, with Marxist parties appearing in Austria, France, Italy, and Switzerland. As I mentioned at the beginning of this book, Marxism was initially created by, and to a certain extent still follows, the work of Engels. It was formulated in the 1880s, shortly after Marx's death, and was already in place in the published version of Engels' funeral address. In works such as *Anti-Dühring* (1878) and *Dialectics of Nature*, published in 1927, Engels boiled down Marx's complex ideas into a handful of core tenets.

After the collapse of the Soviet Union in 1991, some commentators claimed Marx's ideas were dead and buried. Francis Fukuyama wrote an essay, later developed into a book called *The End of History and the Last Man* (1992), which claimed that the success of liberal democracy and market capitalism over all other political systems meant the end of history, a claim he has since withdrawn in the wake of twenty-first-century social protest movements, religious terrorism, and populist politics. In a similar vein, the French conservative and philosopher Chantal Delsol used the mythical story of Icarus – who dared to fly too close to the Sun on wings of feather and wax – to capture the current situation of western humanity, whose reckless search for utopia sent us spiralling back to earth, burned, shaken, and confused (Delsol, 2003). Marx, however, did not envision an authoritarian state. He was a fierce critic of dogma, military terror, and political suppression. It is sadly ironic that Marx, the great theorist of individual freedom, has become associated with the dictatorships of the twentieth century.

MARXIST AESTHETICS

This final section sets out some of the intellectual shifts in Marxism that occurred after Marx's death. Importantly, there is no singular Marxism, but there are multiple Marxisms defined by the allegiance to a specific complex of problems, whose formulations are always in movement and in historic rearrangement and restructuration, along with their object of study (capitalism itself) (Jameson, 2009, 372). Just as capitalism changes, so does Marxism.

Marxist aesthetics is a set of approaches to literature and culture based on the works of Marx. It involves establishing political interventions that ground cultural productions within the historical development of capitalism. More than any other theory, Marxist aesthetics has a unique ability to read literature and culture in relation to the structural contradictions of capitalism, and to create an alternative critical vision. Engels, for instance, argued that he had learned more about French society from Balzac 'than from all the professed historians, economists and statisticians of the period together' (*MECW48*, 168). Balzac, for all his criticism of the French middle class, was motivated by a desire to retain monarchy. But Balzac's extensive studies of the period powerfully revealed these contradictions, compelling him, as Engels argued, to go against 'his own class sympathies and political prejudices' (*ibid.*, 168). As Engels wrote, 'his satire is never keener, his irony never bitterer, than when he sets in motion the very men and women with whom he sympathizes most deeply – the nobles' (*ibid.*). Marxist aesthetics need not just pay attention to texts dealing with the working class, revolution, or communism, but can construct powerful modes of criticism by reading texts that do not discuss any of these issues.

Marxist aesthetics includes figures as diverse as Georg Lukács (1885–1971), Theodor Adorno (1903–1969), Bertolt Brecht (1898–1956), Herbert Marcuse (1898–1979), Walter Benjamin (1892–1940), Louis Althusser (1918–1990), Pierre Macherey (1938–), Gayatri Chakravorty Spivak (1942–), Stuart Hall (1932–2014), Raymond Williams (1921–1988), Terry Eagleton (1943–), Jodi Dean (1962–), and Fredric Jameson (1934–). Many of these figures have been discussed in the *Routledge Critical Thinkers* series, and so in the space available I will direct your attention to these guides. Given the inconclusive and often ambiguous nature of Marx's and Engels' comments on literature and culture, subsequent generations of Marxist intellectuals have empathised with different aspects of critical enquiry. This tradition is exciting, but unpicking individual strands can be difficult. The following furnishes a useful overview for those of you who wish to pursue this intellectual tradition further.

CLASSICAL MARXISM

Classical Marxism refers to the work of Marx and Engels. Even today, the complete writings of these two philosophers are still being uncovered and published in scholarly editions. This international collected works project is almost complete, but it will be some time before the new editions are rendered into English. The continued discovery of new manuscripts is clear evidence that we have not yet come to terms with everything Marx and Engels wrote. What followed in the first half of the twentieth century was the ossification of Marx's ideas into party-political dogma. Marxism-Leninism, named after the life and work of the Russian revolutionary Vladimir Lenin (1870–1924), was an appalling impoverishment of Marx's work. This new system presented itself like a religion, conferring a secret wisdom that was compelling in its purity. As the philosopher Bertrand Russell remarked of the political repression and mass killings carried out by the Bolshevik party, the 'price mankind must pay to achieve communism by Bolshevik methods is too terrible' (Russell, 1964, 101).

THE FRANKFURT SCHOOL

The major exception to this was the work of the Frankfurt School. This institute was founded on 3rd February 1923 at the University of Frankfurt, and continues today, but the term really refers to a small group of scholars in exile after 1933 and their work on a critical theory of society. Members and affiliates of the Frankfurt school included Max Horkheimer, Theodor Adorno, Herbert Marcuse, Erich Fromm, and Walter Benjamin. The work of the Frankfurt School was grounded in a plural Marxism which took as its subject social existence under consumer capitalism. The depth and range of their works represents one of the most collaborative and sophisticated efforts in the Marxist critical and dialectical tradition.

STRUCTURAL MARXISM

In the period after the Second World War, particularly in France, Marxism was influenced by structuralism (a set of ideas that proposes culture must be understood in relation to broader, overreaching systems or structures). Important works were produced by Étienne Balibar (1942–) and Pierre Macherey (1938–), but the most important were books by Althusser and Balibar (1918–1990): *For Marx* (1965) and *Reading Capital* (1965) (Althusser, 2005; Althusser and Balibar, 2009). In the former, Althusser proposed an 'epistemological break' or rupture between the young and mature Marx. Althusser argued Marx's early works were filled with Hegelian philosophy. In contrast, Marx's mature writings, chiefly his turn to a critique of political economy, represented the creation of a genuine scientific knowledge. Influential at the time, this reading has been widely attacked, with scholars identifying points of continuity between the two 'sets' of writings. The last major work of this period is Jameson's *Marxism and Form* (1971), which examined major European Marxist theorists – Adorno, Benjamin, Marcuse, Lukács, Ernst Bloch, and Jean-Paul Sartre – in relation to aesthetic form.

POST-MARXISM

In the 1980s, Marxism morphed into new configurations, driven by post-structuralism and deconstruction. Ernesto Laclau (1935–2014) and Chantal Mouffe (1943–) claimed a 'post-Marxist' approach in their co-authored work *Hegemony and Socialist Strategy* (1985), which rejected class, totality, and production for the concerns of language, discourse, and new social protest movements. Jacques Derrida (1930–2004) wrote a book called *Spectres of Marx* (1993), which read Marx through a series of ghostly demarcations, proposing that the German philosopher continued to haunt capitalism and that we could return to the spirit of Marx if not the letter (Derrida, 2006, 11).

CONTEMPORARY MARXISM

Michael Hardt and Antonio Negri wrote an important trilogy of works: *Empire* (2000), *Multitude* (2004), and *Commonwealth*

(2006), which respond to the economic and geopolitical development of globalisation from a Marxist standpoint. More recently, Aaron Bastani has argued that new automation technologies will create a post-work society of communal luxury which he optimistically calls *Fully Automated Luxury Communism* (2019). For Bastani, previous modes of production were unsuitable to automation, meaning a communist politics has not been possible until now.

In contemporary culture, Marxist critical approaches remain open and plural, constantly seeking to enrich our understanding of literature and culture as vital sources of experience while risking ever-greater exposure to new and ever-developing fields of knowledge. The single most pathbreaking effort is the American Marxist Fredric Jameson's six volume study *The Poetics of Social Forms*. These are a series of works which provide a history of western aesthetics in relation to Marxist political and cultural criticism. Marx's work in the field of cultural criticism is provisional but continues to offer rich interpretive resources and possibilities. Terry Eagleton has produced a number of major works across the past 40 years, providing engaging introductions to literary theory and culture which are best treated together. These include *Literary Theory* (1983), *After Theory* (2004), and *How to Read Literature* (2014). His prominent works on Marx and Marxism are *Why Marx was Right* (2011) and *Marxism and Literary Criticism* (1976).

There is much that Marx left out. His accounts of capitalism did not explore race, sex, gender, or ethnicity in any sustained manner. Nor did Marx demarcate what a communist society looks like. Most importantly, he never completed *Capital*. Nevertheless, Marx is the most important thinker of modern times. None of the attacks on his work has been able to provide methods for generating the depth of insight that Marx could achieve. His works, and the spirit of his critique, will continue to be relevant for as long as capitalism exists. But we need a way of assessing not just what is wrong about capitalism, but what is desirable about alternatives to it. Climate action groups, cooperatives, volunteering, freecycling, ethical shopping, free software, online courses, platform cooperatives, collective agency, community, solidarity, and trade unionism all help shake us out from the logics of capitalist enterprise, if only in a small and sometimes momentary way.

Marx is a rare thinker, one who changed the way we see the world. To appreciate Marx fully requires familiarity with his diverse writings. To read Marx is to clarify our understanding of society. It can also change the world.

FURTHER READING

The Works Cited section at the end of this book includes the complete list of works that appear in this volume.

COLLECTED WRITINGS AND COMPANIONS

Marx's output was enormous. There are two major editions of Marx's collected works. The first is the *Marx/Engels Collected Works* (*MECW*), published by Lawrence & Wishart. The *MECW* is the largest existing collection, in English, of most of the works by Marx and Engels. The collected works comprise fifty volumes, compiled and issued from 1975 to 2004. The *MECW* is the most comprehensive collection of works to date, but it is not the entire works. The second is the *Marx/Engels Gesamtausgabe* (*MEGA*), which is a scholarly effort to collect all of Marx and Engel's writings. While there are problems with the first collected works project, and the second only appears in German, what follows is a select list of some of the most important works.

Marx and Engels Collected Works (*MECW*), 50 volumes (London: Lawrence & Wishart, 1975–2005). The definitive English language edition of Marx and Engels' writings.

It contains all of the major works by both philosophers, plus manuscripts and letters.

Karl Marx Friedrich Engels Gesamtausgabe (*MEGA*), prospectively 120 volumes (Dietz Verlag, 1975–98, then Akademie Verlag, 1998–). The largest collection of the writings of Marx and Engels in any language. It is still an ongoing project, aiming to establish a critical edition of the complete works of the two thinkers. All the material is in the original language, so it is only really of use for German speakers.

The Bloomsbury Companion to Marx, edited by Andrew Pendakis, Imre Szeman and Jeff Diamanti (London: Bloomsbury, 2018). A major reference guide to Marx's life, context, works, and sources. Chapters cover key texts, themes, and concepts.

Karl Marx: Selected Writings, second edition, edited by David McLellan (Oxford: Oxford University Press, 2000). A very useful guide to the important works of Marx, with commentary by a major Marxist thinker.

Karl Marx: A Reader, edited by Jon Elster (Cambridge: Cambridge University Press, 1986). A selection of Marx's major writings organised under thematic headings such as alienation, ideology, and historical materialism.

WORKS BY MARX

Karl Marx and Erich Fromm, *Marx's Concept of Man: Including 'Economic and Philosophical Manuscripts'* (London: Bloomsbury, 2013). A useful introduction to the manuscripts from a former member of the Frankfurt School.

Karl Marx and Friedrich Engels, the *Communist Manifesto* (Oxford: Oxford University Press, 1992). The best and most readable translation in English. Contains a useful introduction and critical commentary.

Karl Marx and Friedrich Engels, *The German Ideology*, edited and introduced by Christopher John Arthur (London: Lawrence &

Wishart, 1970). The full text is massive, so this is a useful 'student' text which contains an excellent introduction and the most important parts of the work.

Karl Marx and Friedrich Engels, *The German Ideology: Including Theses on Feuerbach and an Introduction to the Critique of Political Economy* (New York: Prometheus Books, 1998). Presents the full work along with images of the original manuscript (in Marx's terrible handwriting).

Karl Marx, *Capital: A Critique of Political Economy*, Volume 1, trans. by Ben Fowkes (London: Penguin, 1990). The best and most commonly used edition of Marx's master work. It contains an introduction by the Marxist economist Ernest Mandel, along with the many prefaces to the different editions of *Capital*.

Karl Marx, *Grundrisse: Foundations of the Critique of Political Economy (Rough Draft)*, trans. by Martin Nicolaus (London: Penguin, 1993). This is the first draft of *Capital* and is made up of the notebooks on capital and money that Marx wrote after the financial crisis of 1857. This is the full text with a useful introduction.

Karl Marx, *The Political Writings*, introduced by David Fernbach (London & New York: Verso, 2019). This work collects all of the shorter pieces by Marx, including the *Communist Manifesto*, *The Eighteenth Brumaire of Louis Bonaparte*, *The Class Struggles in France*, and *The Critique of the Gotha Programme*, with introductions on the period.

WORKS BY ENGELS

Friedrich Engels, *The Condition of the Working Class in England* (Oxford: Oxford World Classics, 2009). While living and working in Manchester, Engels documented the terrible living conditions of factory workers, demanding radical change.

Friedrich Engels, *Anti-Dühring: Herr Eugen Dühring's Revolution in Science* (London: Martin Lawrence, 1934). Often referred to as the first 'Marxist' text, Engels wrote the work to respond to Professor Eugen Dühring's version of socialism. Part of it was published as *Socialism: Utopian and Scientific*.

Friedrich Engels, *Dialectics of Nature* (Moscow: Progress Publishers, 1966). An unfinished work by Engels that applies dialectical materialism to science.

WORKS BY HEGEL

Georg Wilhelm Friedrich Hegel, *The Hegel Reader*, edited by Stephen Houlgate (Oxford: Blackwell, 1998). An impressive collection of Hegel's major writings.

Georg Wilhelm Friedrich Hegel, *The Science of Logic*, translated and edited by George di Giovanni (Cambridge: Cambridge University Press, 2015). Hegel presents his system of dialectics, which examines becoming, existence, reality, and essence.

Georg Wilhelm Friedrich Hegel, *Introductory Lectures on Aesthetics*, translated by Bernard Bosanquet, edited by Michael Inwood (London: Penguin Books, 1993). A copy of Hegel's lectures given in Berlin in the 1820s.

Georg Wilhelm Friedrich Hegel, *The Phenomenology of Spirit*, translated and edited by Terry Pinkard (Cambridge: Cambridge University Press, 2018). Hegel's major work, with an introduction and commentary by a leading Hegel scholar.

FURTHER READING ON HEGEL

Dean Moyar (ed.), *The Oxford Handbook to Hegel* (New York: Oxford University Press 2017). A comprehensive guide to Hegel's work. Includes numerous chapters on *The Phenomenology, The Science of Logic*, and the lectures.

Alexandre Kojève, *Lectures on the Phenomenology of Spirit*, assembled by Raymond Queneau; edited by Allan Bloom; translated from the French by James H. Nichols, Jr (Ithaca: Cornell University Press, 1980). A path-breaking reading of Hegel, which also brings in the work of Marx.

Horst Althaus, *Hegel: An Intellectual Biography*, translated by Michael Tarsh (Cambridge: Polity Press, 2000). Anchors Hegel in the German intellectual tradition. Accessible and highly readable.

Terry Pinkard, *Hegel: A Biography* (Cambridge: Cambridge University Press, 2001). The major biography of Hegel, which captures the importance of his life and thought in lively prose.

Michael Inwood, *A Hegel Dictionary* (Oxford: Blackwell 1992). An explanation of the major terms that Hegel created and used in his work. A very useful tool for anyone reading Hegel.

Charles Taylor, *Hegel* (Cambridge: Cambridge University Press, 1975). First published in 1965, but still a major and impressive work of scholarship which introduces Hegel's life and his major ideas.

Karl Marx, *Critique of Hegel's Philosophy of Right* (1843)

BIOGRAPHIES OF MARX

David McLellan, *Karl Marx: His Life and Thought* (London: Macmillan, 1973). A very detailed biography of Marx by a major Marxist thinker.

Jonathan Sperber, *Karl Marx: A Nineteenth-Century Life* (New York and London: Liveright Publishing, 2013). A well-researched and written account of Marx's life, but arguing that Marx never escaped the limitations of a nineteenth century worldview.

Gareth Stedman Jones, *Karl Marx: Greatness and Illusion* (London: Penguin Books, 2017). A very detailed reading of Marx and the intellectual period in which he wrote. Marx's work is positioned in dialogue with other contemporary figures.

Sven-Eric Liedman, *A World to Win: The Life and Thought of Karl Marx* (London: Verso Books, 2018). An impressive and detailed account of Marx's life, which shows his originality and relevance for today.

Mary Gabriel, *Love and Capital: Karl and Jenny Marx and the Birth of a Revolution* (London: Little, Brown, 2012). An accessible and moving reading of the relationship between Marx and his wife Jenny. It remains attentive to Marx the man, representing him as in part prankster, husband, father, and committed revolutionary.

Francis Wheen, *Karl Marx* (London: Fourth Estate, 1999). An informative and light account of Marx's life. It is a little bit 'journalistic' in part and does not really engage with the critical aspects of Marx's work.

POPULAR CULTURE

Rupert Woodfin and Oscar Zarate, *Marxism: A Graphic Guide* (London: Icon Books, 2018). A fun and engaging overview of Marx and Marxism.

Martin Rowson, *The Communist Manifesto: A Graphic Novel* (London: SelfMadeHero, 2018). A detailed graphic representation of Marx's most famous text.

David N. Smith and Phil Evans, *Marx's Capital: An Illustrated Introduction* (London: Haymarket Books, 2014). A graphic introduction to the core aspects of Marx's critical theory. Introduces capital, the commodity, money, labour, and class struggle.

Kat Evans, *Red Rosa: A Graphic Biography of Rosa Luxemburg* (London: Verso, 2015). A graphic life of one of the most important twentieth-century Marxist figures, the Polish-born philosopher Rosa Luxemburg. It also introduces some of Marx's key ideas through engaging illustrations. A remarkable text which is also a wonderful story.

READERS ON *CAPITAL*

Fredric Jameson, *Representing Capital: A Reading of Volume 1* (London: Verso, 2014). Jameson is the foremost Marxist thinker living today, and this slim book offers impressive readings of Marx's most famous text. It can be hard going, but definitely worth the effort.

David Harvey, *A Companion to Marx's Capital* (London: Verso, 2010). An excellent primer for reading Marx's text. Harvey takes us through the core concepts, including commodity, value, exchange, and so on. It is useful to first read the relevant section in Marx's work, then use Harvey to provide an explanation.

Alex Callinicos, *Deciphering Capital* (London: Bookmarks Publications, 2014). Neither a guide nor an introduction to *Capital*. Callinicos is interested in exploring Marx's method and its connection to Hegelian philosophy.

Slavoj Žižek, Frank Ruda, and Agon Hamza, *Reading Marx* (London: Polity Press, 2018). Written by three prominent philosophers, this book reads Marx through Hegel and Lacan to produce some innovative insights. It is particularly concerned with establishing new forms of emancipatory politics anchored in Marx's original texts.

Ingo Schmidt and Carlo Fanelli (eds), *Reading Capital Today: Marx After 150 Years* (London: Pluto Press, 2017). A brilliant collection of essays interested in Marx's philosophy and political economy. Includes chapters on *Capital* in relation to gender, race, class, ecology, and communism.

MARXIST POLITICAL ECONOMY

Joseph Choonara, *Unravelling Capitalism: A Guide to Marxist Political Economy*, second edition (London: Bookmarks, 2017). A short, accessible guide to Marx's ideas on capitalism, showing how capital is a system geared towards exploitation, instability, and repeated crisis.

David Harvey, *A Brief History of Neoliberalism* (Oxford: Oxford University Press, 2007). A superb introduction to a new ideology of market-oriented ethics that has been on the rise since the 1970s.

David Harvey, *Seventeen Contradictions and the End of Capitalism* (London: Profile Books, 2014). Harvey explores the multiple contradictions of capitalism, showing how capitalism is a system that appears eternal while constantly operating on the verge of collapse. Chapters are short, detailed, and well-written.

David Harvey, *Marx, Capital and the Madness of Economic Reason* (London: Profile, 2017). Exploring the architecture of Marx's *Capital*, Harvey focuses on Marx's presentation of capital as something constantly in motion and change.

MARXISM AND NATURE

John Bellamy Foster, *Marx's Ecology: Materialism and Nature* (New York and London: Monthly Review Press, 1999). An immensely important study that overturns the long-held assessment that Marx was a thinker more interested in economy than ecology. It excavates and examines Marx's neglected writings on nature, agriculture, soil, philosophical naturalism, and evolutionary theory.

John Bellamy Foster and Paul Burkett, *Marx and the Earth: An Anti-Critique* (Leiden: Brill, 2016). A response to eco-socialist criticisms of Marx. The book explores dialectics, ecological economics, and theories of thermodynamics and entropy to argue for a new green revolutionary politics.

Paul Burkett, *Marxism and Ecological Economics: Toward a Red and Green Political Economy* (Chicago: Haymarket Books, 2009). Burkett uses Marx's writings on capital to show how Marxist theories can contribute to ecological economics – that is, a mode of economics that seeks to promote human flourishing and environmental sustainability. Chapters cover nature and economic value, the treatment of nature as capital, the significance of entropy, and the idea of sustainable development.

Paul Burkett, *Marx and Nature: A Red and Green Perspective* (Chicago: Haymarket Books, 2014). A reconstruction of Marx's ideas about nature, which argues that while Marx thought production was central to human development, he also recognised that production takes place in, and is constrained by, natural conditions. It places Marx within a growing camp of ecological theorists.

Kohei Saito, *Karl Marx's Ecosocialism: Capitalism, Nature, and the Unfinished Critique of Political Economy* (New Delhi: Dev Publishers, 2017). A fascinating reading of newly available documents – Marx's natural science notebooks. Saito goes further than Bellamy Foster and Burkett, arguing that it is not possible to comprehend Marx without taking account of his ecological dimension. An important and timely work for a world wracked by growing environmental crisis and ecological catastrophe.

MARXISM, CLASS, AND INTERSECTIONALITY

Domenico Losurdo, *Class Struggle: A Political and Philosophical History*, translated by Gregory Elliot (London: Palgrave Macmillan, 2016). Reinterprets Marx's writings on class struggle, arguing that while it is typically understood as workers against capitalists, Marx envisioned class struggle as a social conflict. For Losurdo, class struggle goes beyond class, and includes broader forms of political emancipation.

Ashley J. Bohrer, *Marxism and Intersectionality: Race, Gender, Class and Sexuality under Contemporary Capitalism* (Biefield: Transcript, 2019). A long-overdue assessment of the critical relations among Marx, Marxism, race, sex, and gender. Bohrer argues that many of the purported oppositions between Marxism and intersectionality result from miscommunication rather than antagonism. Marxism has a lot to say about the many forms of exploitation and domination within capital.

MARXISM AND COMMUNISM

Bruno Bosteels, *The Actuality of Communism* (London: Verso, 2011). Explores the current revival of interest in communism, reading work by Alain Badiou, Jacques Rancière, and Slavoj Žižek.

Jodi Dean, *The Communist Horizon* (London: Verso, 2012). A reading of communism and recent social protest movements such as Occupy. Dean argues for the importance of the political party over 'spontaneous' protest movements.

Kieran Allan, *Marx and the Alternative to Capitalism* (London: Pluto Press, 2011). A reading of Marx's major works in relation to their importance for constructing a new kind of society, based on the principles of justice, equality, and freedom.

Costas Douzinas and Slavoj Žižek (eds), *The Idea of Communism* (London: Verso, 2010). The collected talks of the 'Idea of Communism' conference held in 2009. Contributions by Alain Badiou, Antoni Negri, Michael Hardt, Jacques Rancière, Terry Eagleton, Jean-Luc Nancy, Susan Buck-Morss, Bruno Bosteels, Peter Hallward, Alberto Toscano, and Wang Hui.

Shannon Brincat, *Communism in the 21st Century*, three volumes (Oxford: Praeger, 2014). A groundbreaking collection that examines the past, present, and future of communism. Chapters examine Marx's communism, twentieth-century communism, and more recent communist movements over the past two decades.

Tom Rockmore, *Marx's Dream: From Capitalism to Communism* (Chicago: University of Chicago Press, 2018). Distinguishes between Marx and Marxism, returning to the original works to explore Marx's vision of a post-capitalist society.

MARX AND ENGELS

Paul Blackledge, *Friedrich Engels and Modern Social and Political Theory* (Albany: SUNY Press, 2019). An engaging reassessment of the work of Engels, focusing on his formation of Marxism after Marx's death, and his contributions to modern political thought.

Terrell Carver, *Engels* (Oxford: Oxford University Press, 1981). One of the first major examinations of the role of the life and work of Engels. Published in the early 1980s, this is still an important and well-argued work.

Terrell Carver, *Marx and Engels: The Intellectual Relationship* (London: Wheatsheaf, 1983). An exploration of the work of the two philosophers and their distinct contributions. While Engels has typically been overshadowed by Marx, Carver argues that Engels played an important role as Marx's literary executor, political heir, and modern interpreter.

Terrell Carver, *Engels before Marx* (London: Palgrave Macmillan, 2020). Examines the life and works of Friedrich Engels during the decade before he entered a political partnership with Karl Marx.

Stephen H. Rigby, *Engels and the Formation of Marxism: History, Dialectics, and Revolution* (Manchester: Manchester University Press, 1992). A critical assessment of the philosophy, social theory, and politics of Marxism. It examines Engels' contribution to the genesis of Marxism in the years before 1848, and the extent to which Engels' later writings departed from his and Marx's outlook of the 1840s.

Kean Kagal, *Friedrich Engels and The Dialectics of Nature* (London: Palgrave, 2020). A detailed examination of one of Engels' most important texts. It analyses Engels' intentions and concerns in writing the book, discusses its reception and editorial history, and examines the unsolved philosophical problems of this unfinished work.

MARXISM AND REVOLUTION

Chris Harman, *Revolution in the 21st Century* (London: Bookmarks, 2007). This short, provocative account explores the critical complexities of revolution, discussing questions such as: Why do revolutions occur? Are revolutions unsuccessful? What do revolutionaries actually think and do?

Hal Draper, *Marx's Theory of Revolution*, Volume 1 (London: Monthly Review Press, 1979). The first of a five-volume discussion of Marx's ideas on revolution, and the ways in which they shifted across his life. Examines Marx's views on democracy, the state, and the roles of intellectuals and revolutionaries.

FURTHER READING IN MARXIST CRITICISM

Terry Eagleton, *Why Marx was Right*, second edition (New Haven and London: Yale University Press, 2018). A powerful defence against the major objections to Marx's work, exploring Marx's ideas in lively and energetic prose to show why his ideas are more relevant today than ever before.

Alex Callinicos, *The Revolutionary Ideas of Karl Marx* (London: Haymarket Books, 2011). An introduction to Marx's key ideas and his commitment to radical social change. Callinicos places Marx's work in dialogue with other thinkers such as Hegel and Ricardo, while also arguing for the originality of Marx's political vision.

Andrew Pendakis, Jeff Diamanit, Nicholas Brown, Josh Robinson, and Imre Szeman, *Contemporary Marxist Theory: A Reader* (London & New York: Bloomsbury Academic, 2014). A collection of essays by key thinkers on Marx and Marxism. Sections cover political economy, cultural studies, literary criticism, and globalisation. Imre Szeman's essay on Marxist literary criticism is particularly insightful.

Marcellu Musto, *Another Marx: Early Manuscripts to the International* (London: Bloomsbury, 2018). Marcello, an excellent scholar of Marx's manuscripts, constructs a critical Marx free from the dogmatism of much of twentieth-century Marxism. He explores Marx's ideas on post-Hegelian philosophy, alienated labour, and the materialist conception of history. A fresh and engaging approach within the new Marx studies.

Leszek Kolakowski, *Main Currents of Marxism*, three volumes (London: W.W. Norton & Company, 2008). A major work of scholarship by a Polish philosopher and critic. Covers all the major schools of Marxist thought, including classical Marxism, Marxism-Leninism, and the Frankfurt School. A detailed treatment of Marx and Marxism, even if some of the analysis could be developed.

MARXIST LITERARY CRITICISM

Terry Eagleton, *Marxism and Literary Criticism* (Routledge: London and New York, 2010). A short, accessible guide to the critical relations between Marx's ideas on class and capital and Marxist literary and cultural criticism. A major work in the field.

Barbara Foley, *Marxist Literary Criticism Today* (London: Pluto Press, 2019). One of the best works on Marxist literary criticism in recent years. Foley focuses on three core concepts: historical materialism, political economy, and ideology, examining texts including Jane Austen's *Pride and Prejudice*, E.L. James' *Fifty Shades of Grey*, Frederick Douglass' 'What to the Slave is the Fourth of July?', Annie Proulx's 'Brokeback Mountain', and W.B. Yeats' 'The Second Coming'. A landmark contribution and essential reading for those interested in Marx, Marxism, and literary criticism.

Fredric Jameson, *Marxism and Form: Twentieth Century Dialectical Theories of Literature* (Princeton: Princeton University Press, 1971). Jameson is the most important Marxist critic living and writing today, and this book, even though more than 50 years old, still makes some stunning, innovative claims. Jameson examines the works of Sartre, Adorno, Lukács, and others, examining dialectics, form, and the connection between aesthetics and history. Reading Jameson is a wonderful experience, not simply for the distinctive nature of his ideas, but for the qualities of his dialectical prose.

Daniel Hartley, *The Politics of Style: Towards a Marxist Poetics* (Leiden: Brill, 2017). Focuses on three major Marxist figures (Fredric Jameson, Terry Eagleton, and Raymond Williams), paying special attention to their construction of a particular style which forms a Marxist poetics. A detailed, complex, and rich account of Marx, literary criticism, and ideology.

S.S. Prawer, *Karl Marx and World Literature* (London: Verso, 2011). Explores how works of imaginative literature helped Marx shape and develop his ideas. Marx was a voracious reader of literary texts, and this book surveys the plays, poems, and stories to which he consistently returned.

WORKS CITED

Adorno, Theodor W., *Hegel: Three Studies*, trans. by Shierry Weber Nicholson (Cambridge, Massachusetts: MIT Press, 1993).

Allen, Kieran, *Marxism and The Alternative to Capitalism* (London: Pluto Press, 2011).

Althusser, Louis, *For Marx* (London: Vintage, 2005).

Althusser, Louis and Étienne Balibar, *Reading Capital*, trans. by Ben Brewster (London & New York: Verso, 2009).

Amin, Samir, *Spectres of Capitalism: A Critique of Current Intellectual Fashions*, 2nd edn, trans. by Shane Henry Mage (New York: Monthly Review Press, 2010).

Anderson, Perry, *Considerations on Western Marxism* (London: Western Printing, 1976).

Anderson, Perry, *In the Tracks of Historical Materialism* (London: Verso, 1983).

Anderson, Perry, *Spectrum: From Right to Left in the World of Ideas* (London: Verso, 2007).

Aristotle, *Poetics* (Oxford: Oxford University Press, 2013).

Aronowitz, Stanley, *The Crisis in Historical Materialism: Class, Politics and Culture in Marxist Theory* (Basingstoke: Macmillan, 1990).

Aronson, Ronald, *After Marxism* (New York: Guilford Press, 1988).

Arthur, Christopher J., 'Contradiction and Abstraction: A reply to Finelli', *Historical Materialism 17* (2009), pp.170–182.

Arthur, Christopher J., *The New Dialectic and Marx's Capital* (Cambridge, Massachusetts: MIT Press, 2000).

Badiou, Alain, *The Communist Hypothesis* (London & New York: Verso, 2015).

Badiou, Alain, *Theory of the Subject* (London: Continuum, 1999).

Badiou, Alain and Slavoj Žižek, 'Have Michael Hardt and Antonio Negri Rewritten the Communist Manifesto for the Twenty-First Century?', *Rethinking Marxism 13.3* (2001), pp.190–198.

Balzac, Honoré de, *The History of the Thirteen* (London: Penguin, 1972).

Bastani, Arin, *Fully Automated Luxury Communism: A Manifesto* (London: Verso, 2019).

Baudrillard, Jean, *The Mirror of Production*, trans. and introduced by Mark Poster (St Louis, Missouri: Telos Press, 1975).

Baudrillard, Jean, *For a Critique of The Political Economy of the Sign*, trans. by Charles Levin (St Louis, Missouri: Telos Press, 1981).

Becker, Wolfgang (director and writer), *Good Bye Lenin!* (X Filme Creative Pool, WDR Westdeutscher Rundfunk, ARTE France, 2003).

Beiser, Frederick, *Hegel* (New York: Routledge, 2005).

Bellofiore, Ricardo, Guido Starosta, and Peter D. Thomas, *Marx's Laboratory: Critical Interpretations of the Grundrisse* (Leiden: Brill, 2013).

Berger, John, *Landscapes: John Berger on Art*, edited by Tom Overton (London: Verso, 2016).

Berlant, Lauren, 'Cruel Optimism: On Marx, Loss, and the Senses', *New Formations* 63 (2007), pp.33–51.

Berlin, Isaiah, *The Hedgehog and the Fox: An Essay on Tolstoy's View of History* (Princeton, NJ: Princeton University Press, 2013).

Berman, Marshal, *The Adventures of Marxism* (London: Verso, 2002).

Bidet, Jacques and Stathis Kouvelakis, edited, *Critical Companion to Contemporary Marxism*, Historical Materialism Book Series, Volume 16 (Boston: Brill, 2008).

Blyth, Mark, *Austerity: The History of a Dangerous Idea* (New York & Oxford: Oxford University Press, 2013).

Bogdanov, A., Graham, L.R., Stites, R., and Rougle, C., *Red Star: The First Bolshevik Utopia* (Bloomington, IN: Indiana University Press, 1984).

Bottomore, Tom, edited, *A Dictionary of Marxist Thought* (Oxford: Blackwell, 1987).

Bourg, Julian, *From Revolution to Ethics: May 1968 and Contemporary French Thought* (Montreal & Kingston: McGill-Queens University Press, 2007).

Bowman, Paul, *Post-Marxism versus Cultural Studies: Theory, Politics and Intervention* (Edinburgh: Edinburgh University Press, 2005).

Boxall, Peter, *The Value of the Novel* (New York: Cambridge University Press, 2015).

Breckman, Warren, 'Times of Theory: On Writing the History of French Theory', *Journal of the History of Ideas* 71.3 (2010), pp.339–361.

Breckman, Warren, *Adventures of the Symbolic: Post-Marxism and Radical Democracy* (New York: Columbia University Press, 2013).

Buchanan, Ian, edited, *Jameson on Jameson: Conversations on Cultural Marxism* (Durham & London: Duke University Press, 2007).

Buck-Morss, Susan, *Dreamworld and Catastrophe: The Passing of Mass Utopia in the West* (Boston, Massachusetts: MIT Press, 2002).

Budgen, Sebastian, Stathis Kouvelakis and Slavoj Žižek, edited, *Lenin Reloaded: Toward a Politics of Truth* (Durham: Duke University Press, 2007).

Buhle, Paul, *Marxism in the United States* (London: Verso, 2013).

Burkett, Paul, *Marx and Nature: A Red and Green Perspective* (London: Haymarket, 2014).

Butler, Judith, Ernesto Laclau and Slavoj Žižek, *Contingency, Hegemony and Universality: Contemporary Dialogues on the Left* (London: Verso, 2011).

Byron, Glennis and David Punter, edited, *Spectral Readings: Towards a Gothic Geography* (Basingstoke: Macmillan, 1999).

Callinicos, Alex, *Against Postmodernism: A Marxist Critique* (Cambridge: Polity, 1989).

Callinicos, Alex, *The Revenge of History: Marxism and the East European Revolutions* (University Park, Pennsylvania: Penn State University Press, 1991).

Callinicos, Alex, *The Revolutionary Ideas of Karl Marx* (Chicago: Haymarket, 2010).

Callinicos, Alex, *Deciphering Capital: Marx's Capital and its Destiny* (London: Bookmarks, 2014).

Carroll, Hamilton and Annie McClanahan, 'Fictions of Speculation: Introduction', *Journal of American Studies 49.4* (2015), pp.655–661.

Carswell, Sean, *Occupy Pynchon: Politics after Gravity's Rainbow* (Athens, GA: University of Georgia Press, 2017).

Carver, Terrell, 'Marx's Eighteenth Brumaire of Louis Bonaparte—Eliding 150 Years', *Strategies: Journal of Theory, Politics & Culture 16.1* (2003), pp.5–11.

Chandor, J.C. (director and writer), *Margin Call* (Before the Door Pictures, Benaroya Pictures, Washington Square Films, 2011).

Claeys, Gregory, edited, *The Cambridge Companion to Utopian Literature* (Cambridge: Cambridge University Press, 2010).

Claeys, Gregory, *Dystopia: A Natural History* (Oxford: Oxford University Press, 2018).

Clark, John P., 'Marx's Inorganic Body', *Environmental Ethics 11.3* (1989) pp.243–58.

Clark, Terry Nichols and Seymour Martin Lipset, edited, *The Breakdown of Class Politics: A Debate on Post-Industrial Stratification* (Baltimore: John Hopkins University Press, 2001).

Clarke, Arthur C., edited, *Profiles of the Future: An Inquiry into the Limits of the Possible* (London: Indigo, 2000).

Cohen, Emily Jane, 'Museums of the Mind: The Gothic and the Art of Memory', *ELH 62.4* (1995), pp.883–905.

Cohen, Margaret, *Profane Illumination: Walter Benjamin and the Paris of Surrealist Revolution* (Berkley: University of California Press, 1993).

Coole, Diana and Samantha Frost, edited, *New Materialisms: Ontology, Agency, and Politics* (Durham & London: Duke University Press, 2010).

Cooper, Luke and Simon Hardy, *Beyond Capitalism? The Future of Radical Politics* (London: Zero Books, 2012).

Cowart, David, *Thomas Pynchon & the Dark Passages of History* (Athens & London: University of Georgia Press, 2011).

Cox, Laurence and Alf Gunvald Nilsen, *We Make Our Own History: Marxism and Social Movements in the Twilight of Neoliberalism* (London: Pluto Press, 2014).

Crutzen, Paul, 'Geology of Mankind', *Nature 415*, p.23 (2002), https://doi.org/10.1038/415023a

Davies, William, *The Limits to Neoliberalism: Authority, Sovereignty and the Logic of Competition* (London: Sage, 2014).

Davies, William, 'The New Neoliberalism', *New Left Review 101*, September–October (2016).

Dean, Jodi, *The Communist Horizon* (London: Verso, 2012).

Dean, Jodi, 'The Question of Organization', *South Atlantic Quarterly 113.4* (2014), pp.821–835.

Dean, Jodi, *Crowds and Party* (London & New York: Verso, 2016).

Dean, Jodi, *Comrade: An Essay on Political Belonging* (London & New York: Verso, 2019).

Deckard, Shane, Nicholas Lawrence, Neil Lazarus, Graeme McDonald, Upamanyu Pablo Mukherjee, Benita Perry and Stephen Shapiro, *Combined and Uneven Development: Towards a New Theory of World Literature (Warwick Research Collective)* (Liverpool: Liverpool University Press, 2015).

Deleuze, Gilles, *Foucault*, trans. and edited by Sean Hand (London: Continuum, 1999).

Deleuze, Gilles and Félix Guattari, *A Thousand Plateaus: Capitalism and Schizophrenia* (London: Bloomsbury, 1988).

Dellamora, Richard, edited, *Postmodern Apocalypse: Theory and Cultural Practice at the End* (Philadelphia: University of Pennsylvania Press, 1995).

Delsol, Chantal, *Icarus Fallen: The Search for Meaning in an Uncertain World* (Wilmington, DE: ISI Books, 2003).

Demetz, Peter, *Marx, Engels and the Poets: Origins of Marxist Literary Criticism*, trans. by Jeffrey L. Sammons (Chicago: University of Chicago Press, 1967).

Derrida, Jacques, *Spectres of Marx: The State of Debt, the Work of Mourning, and the New International* (London: Routledge, 2006).

Dreiser, Theodore, *Sister Carrie* (London: Penguin, 1981).

Douzinas, Costas and Slavoj Žižek, *The Idea of Communism* (London & New York: Verso, 2010).

Eagleton, Terry, *After Theory* (London: Penguin, 2004).

Eagleton, Terry, *Marxism and Literary Criticism* (London & New York: Routledge, 2010).

Eagleton, Terry, *Why Marx was Right* (New Haven & London: Yale University Press, 2011).

Elliott, Gregory, *Ends in Sight: Marx/Fukuyama/Hobsbawm/Anderson* (London: Pluto, 2008).

Engels, Friedrich, *The Condition of the Working Class in England* (Oxford: Oxford World Classics, 2009).

Ferguson, Iain, *Politics of the Mind: Marxism and Mental Distress* (London: Bookmarks, 2017).

Fisher, Mark, *Capitalist Realism: Is There No Alternative?* (Ropley, UK: Zer0 Books, 2009).

Foley, Barbara, *Marxist Literary Criticism Today* (London: Pluto Press, 2019).

Foster, John Bellamy, *Marx's Ecology: Materialism and Nature* (New York: Monthly Review Press, 2000).

Foster, John Bellamy, Brett Clark and Richard York, edited, *The Ecological Rift: Capitalism's War on the Earth* (New York: Monthly Review Press, 2011).

Fukuyama, Francis, 'The End of History?' *National Interest* 16 (1989), pp.3–18.

Fukuyama, Francis, *The End of History and the Last Man* (London: Penguin, 1992).

Fulbrook, Mary, *Anatomy of a Dictatorship: Inside the GDR 1949–1989* (New York: Oxford University Press, 1995).

Furet, François, *In the Workshop of History*, trans. by Jonathan Mandelbaum (Chicago: University of Chicago Press, 1985).

Geras, Norman, *Marx and Human Nature* (London: New Left Books, 1983).

Geras, Norman, 'Ex-Marxism without Substance: Being a Reply to Laclau and Mouffe', *New Left Review 1.169* (1988), pp.34–61.

Ghodsee, Kristen, *Why Women Have Better Sex Under Socialism, And Other Arguments for Economic Independence* (London: The Bodley Head, 2018).

Gibson, William and Bruce Sterling, *The Difference Engine* (London: Vista, 1991).

Gibson-Graham, J.K., *A Postcapitalist Politics* (Minneapolis: University of Minnesota Press, 2006).

Gill, Stephen, 'The Global Panopticon? The Neoliberal State, Economic Life, and Democratic Surveillance', *Alternatives: Global, Local, Political 20.1* (1995), pp.1–49.

Glocer, Fiorini, Leticia Thierry Bokanowski and Sergio Lewkowicz Melgar, edited, *On Freud's 'Mourning and Melancholia'* (London: Karnac Books, 2009).

Goldstein, Philip, *Post-Marxist Theory: An Introduction* (Albany: New York University Press, 2005).

Gorz, Andre, *Farwell to the Working Class: An Essay on Post-Industrial Socialism*, trans. by Mike Sonenscher (London, Pluto Press, 1982).

Gottfried, Paul E., *The Strange Death of Marxism: The European Left in the New Millennium* (Columbia, Missouri: University of Missouri Press, 2005).

Graham, Hugh Davis and Ted Robert Gurr, edited, *The History of Violence in America* (New York: Praeger, 1969).

Gramsci, Antonio, *Selections from The Prison Notebooks*, edited and trans. by Quintin Hoare and Geoffrey Nowell-Smith (London: Lawrence & Wishart, 1971).

Gramsci, Antonio, *The Politics of Thatcherism*, edited by Stuart Hall and Martin Jacques (London: Lawrence & Wishart, 1983).

Gramsci, Antonio, *The Hard Road to Renewal: Thatcherism and the Crisis of the Left* (London: Verso, 1988).

Hardt, Michael and Antonio Negri, *Empire* (Cambridge, Massachusetts: Harvard University Press, 2000).

Hardt, Michael and Antonio Negri, *Multitude: War and Democracy in the Age of Empire* (London & New York: Penguin, 2006).

Hardt, Michael and Antonio Negri, *Commonwealth* (Cambridge, Massachusetts: Harvard University Press, 2009).

Harvey, David, *A Brief History of Neoliberalism* (Oxford: Oxford University Press, 2007).

Harvey, David, *A Companion to Marx's Capital* (London & New York: Verso, 2010).

Harvey, David, *The Enigma of Capital and the Crisis of Capitalism* (London: Profile, 2011).

Harvey, David, *Seventeen Contradictions and the End of Capitalism* (London: Profile, 2014).

Hegel, Georg Wilhelm Fredrich, *Lectures on the Philosophy of World History*, trans. by H.B. Nisbet (Cambridge: Cambridge University Press, 1975).

Hegel, Georg Wilhelm Fredrich, *Phenomenology of Spirit*, trans. by A.V. Miller (New York: Oxford University Press, 1977).

Hegel, Georg Wilhelm Friedrich, *The Phenomenology of Spirit*, trans. and ed. by Terry Pinkard (Cambridge: Cambridge University Press, 2018).

Hegel, Georg Wilhelm Fredrich, *The Science of Logic*, trans. and edited by George di Giovanni (Cambridge: Cambridge University Press, 2015).

Heinrich, Michael. 'The "Fragment on Machines": A Marxian Misconception in the *Grundrisse* and its Overcoming in Capital', in *Marx's Laboratory: Critical Interpretations of the Grundrisse*, edited by R. Bellofiore, G. Starosta, and P. Thomas, pp.197–212 (Leiden: Brill, 2013).

Hillman, Roger, 'Goodbye Lenin (2003): History in the subjunctive', *Rethinking History 10.2* (2006) pp.221–37, DOI: 10.1080/13642520600648558

Hindess, Barry, *Politics and Class Analysis* (Oxford: Blackwell, 1987).

Hindess, Barry, *The Decline of Working Class Politics* (London: Granada, 1971).

Hindess, Barry and Paul Q. Hirst, *Pre-Capitalist Modes of Production* (London: Routledge & Kegan Paul, 1975).

Hindess, Barry and Paul Q. Hirst, *Mode of Production and Social Formation* (London: Macmillan, 1977).

Hobsbawm, Eric, *Age of Extremes: The Short Twentieth Century, 1914–1991* (London: Abacus, 1995).

Holloway, J. (2015) 'Read Capital: The First Sentence, Or Capital Starts with Wealth, not with the Commodity' *Historical Materialism 23.3* pp.3–26.

Hudis, Peter, *Marx's Concept of the Alternative to Capitalism* (Chicago: Haymarket Books, 2012).

Huehls, Mitchum, 'The Great Flattening', *Contemporary Literature 54.4* (2013), pp.861–871.

Hutcheon, Linda, *The Politics of Postmodernism*, second edition (London & New York: Routledge, 2002).

Jameson, Fredric, *Marxism and Form: Twentieth-Century Dialectical Theories of Literature* (Princeton: Princeton University Press, 1971).

Jameson, Fredric, *The Ideologies of Theory,* (London: Verso, 2008).

Jameson, Fredric, *The Political Unconscious: Narrative as a Socially Symbolic Act* (London: Routledge, 1989).

Jameson, Fredric, *The Seeds of Time* (New York: Columbia University Press, 1994).

Jameson, Fredric, *A Singular Modernity: Essay on the Ontology of the Present* (London: Verso, 2002).

Jameson, Fredric, *Late Marxism: Adorno, or the Persistence of the Dialectic* (London: Verso, 2007).

Jameson, Fredric, *Postmodernism Or, The Cultural Logic of Late Capitalism* (London & New York: Verso, 1991).

Jameson, Fredric, *Valences of the Dialectic* (London & New York: Verso, 2009).

Jameson, Fredric, *The Antinomies of Realism* (London: Verso, 2013)

Jameson, Fredric, *Representing Capital: A Reading of Volume One* (London: Verso, 2014).

Jameson, Fredric, *Raymond Chandler: The Detections of Totality* (London: Verso, 2016).

Janzen, David, 'Void of Debt: Crisis and the Remaking of Indebtedness', *Mediations: Journal of the Marxist Literary Group 26.1* (2012), pp.187–193.

Jay, Martin, *The Dialectical Imagination: A History of the Frankfurt School and the Institute of Social Research, 1923–1950* (Berkeley, California & London: University of California Press, 1996).

Johnson, Mark Anthony and Abdullah Mamun, 'The Failure of Lehman Brothers and its Impact on other Financial Institutions', *Financial Economics 22.5* (2012), pp.375–385.

Jones, Owen, *Chavs: The Demonization of the Working Class* (London: Verso, 2012).

Kingston, Paul, *The Classless Society* (Stanford, CA: Stanford University Press, 2001).

Klein, Naomi, *The Shock Doctrine: The Rise of Disaster Capitalism* (London: Penguin, 2008).

Kojève, Alexandre, *Introduction to the Reading of Hegel: Lectures on the 'Phenomenology of Spirit'*, edited by Allan Bloom, trans. by James H. Nichols, Jr. (Ithaca: Cornell University Press, 1980).

Kornbluh, Anne, 'On Marx's Victorian Novel', *Mediations*, *25.1* (2010), pp.15–38.

Kornbluh, Anne, *Realizing Capital: Financial and Psychic Economies in Victorian Form* (New York: Fordham University Press, 2014).

Laclau, Ernesto and Chantal Mouffe, *Hegemony and Socialist Strategy* (London & New York: Verso, 1985).

Laffey, Mark and Kathryn Dean, 'A Flexible Marxism for Flexible Times', in *Historical Materialism and Globalisation: Essays on Continuity and Change*, Mark Rupert and Hazel Smith, eds (London: Routledge, 2016), pp.90–110.

Lane, Richard J., *Jean Baudrillard*, Routledge Critical Thinkers (London: Routledge, 2008).

Lukács, Georg, *History and Class Consciousness: Studies in Marxist Dialectics* (London: Merlin, 1971).

Macherey, Pierre, *A Theory of Literary Production* (London: Routledge, 2006).

Marx, Karl, *Capital: A Critique of Political Economy, Volume 1*, trans. by Ben Fowkes (London: Penguin, 1990).

Marx, Karl, *Grundrisse: Foundations of the Critique of Political Economy (Rough Draft)*, trans. by Martin Nicolaus (London: Penguin, 1993).

Marx, Karl, *Surveys from Exile: Political Writings, Volume 2*, introduced by David Fernbach (London & New York: Verso, 2010).

Marx, Karl, *The Political Writings*, introduced by David Fernbach (London & New York: Verso, 2019).

Marx, Karl and Erich Fromm, *Marx's Concept of Man: Including 'Economic and Philosophical Manuscripts'* (London: Bloomsbury, 2013).

Marx, Karl and Friedrich Engels, the *Communist Manifesto* (Oxford: Oxford University Press, 1992).

Marx, Karl and Friedrich Engels, *The German Ideology*, edited and introduced by Christopher John Arthur (London: Lawrence & Wishart, 1970).

Marx, Karl and Friedrich Engels, *The German Ideology: Including Theses on Feuerbach and an Introduction to the Critique of Political Economy* (New York: Prometheus Books, 1998).

Marx, Karl and Friedrich Engels, *Marx and Engels Collected Works, Volume 40, Letters 1856–1859* (London: Lawrence & Wishart, 2010).

McGuigan, Jim, edited, *Raymond Williams on Culture and Society: Essential Writings* (London: Sage, 2014).

MacGregor, David, *The Communist Ideal in Hegel and Marx* (London & New York: Routledge, 2015).

McLellan, David, *Karl Marx: His Life and Thought* (London: Macmillan, 1973).

Melville, Herman, *Billy Budd, Sailor and Selected Tales* (Oxford: Oxford University Press, 2009).

Musto, Marcello, *Another Marx: Early Manuscripts to the International* (London: Bloomsbury Academic, 2018).

Musto, Marcello, *The Last Years of Karl Marx: An Intellectual Biography* (Palo Alto, CA: Stanford University Press, 2020).

Nelson, Carry and Lawrence Grossberg, *Marxism and the Interpretation of Culture* (Basingstoke: Macmillan Education, 1988).

Neocleous, Mark, 'The Political Economy of the Dead: Marx's Vampires', *History of Political Thought*, 14.4 (2003).

Osborne, Peter, *How to Read Marx* (London: W.W. Norton & Company, 2006).

Pakulski, Jan and Malcolm Waters, *The Death of Class* (London: Sage, 1995).

Pendakis, Andrew, Imre Szeman and Jeff Diamanti (eds), *The Bloomsbury Companion to Marx* (London: Bloomsbury, 2018).

Pinkard, Terry, *Hegel: A Biography* (Cambridge: Cambridge University Press, 2001).

Prawer, S.S., *Karl Marx and World Literature* (London: Verso, 2011).

Roberts, William Clare, *Marx's Inferno: The Political Theory of Capital* (Princeton, NJ, Princeton University Press, 2017).

Rooney, Sally, *Normal People* (London: Faber & Faber, 2018).

Rowcroft, A. 'Editorial: What's Left? Marxism, Literature and Culture in the 21st Century', *Open Library of Humanities*, 5.1 (2019) pp.1–9, DOI: https://doi.org/10.16995/olh.426

Russell, Bertrand, *The Practice and Theory of Bolshevism* (New York: Simon & Schuster, 1964).

Ryan, Frances, *Crippled: Austerity and the Demonization of Disabled People* (London: Verso 2019).

Saito, Kohei, *Karl Marx's Ecosocialism: Capital, Nature, and the Unfinished Critique of Political Economy* (New York: Monthly Review Press, 2017).

Savage, Mike, *Social Class in the 21st Century* (London: Pelican, 2015).

Stallybrass, Peter, 'Marx's Coat', in *Border Fetishisms: Material Objects in Unstable Spaces*, edited by Patricia Spyer (New York: Routledge, 1998), pp.183–207.

Ste Croix, G.E.M. de, *The Class Struggle in the Ancient World* (London: Duckworth, 1983).

Stedman Jones, Gareth, *Karl Marx: Greatness and Illusion* (London: Penguin Books, 2017).

Stuckler, David and Sanjay Basu, *The Body Economic: Why Austerity Kills* (New York: Basic Books, 2013).

Sunkara, Bhaskar, *The Socialist Manifesto: The Case for Radical Politics in an Era of Extreme Inequality* (New York: Hachette, 2019).

Szeman, Imre, 'Marxism after Marxism', *Mediations 24.1* (2008), pp.190–197.

Taylor, Charles, *Hegel* (Cambridge: Cambridge University Press, 1975).

Therborn, Goran, *From Marxism to Post-Marxism* (London: Verso, 2010).

Thoburn, Nicholas, 'Do not be afraid, join us, come back? On the "Idea of Communism" in our time', *Cultural Critique 84.1* (2013), pp.1–34.

Tomba, Massimiliano, *Marx's Temporalities*, trans. Peter D. Thomas and Sara R. Farris (Chicago: Haymarket Books, 2013)

Tomlinson, George, Marx and the concept of historical time, PhD thesis, Kingston University, London, 2015.

Weiss, Peter, *The Aesthetics of Resistance*, Volume 1, trans. by Joachim Neugroschel (Durham: Duke University Press, 2005).

Williams, Raymond, 'Base and Superstructure in Marxist Cultural Theory', *New Left Review 1.82* (1973).

Wright, Erik Olin, *Class Counts* (Cambridge: Cambridge University Press, 2010).

Wright, Erik Olin, *Understanding Class* (London: Verso, 2015).

Žižek, Slavoj, 'A Plea for Leninist Intolerance', *Critical Enquiry 28.2* (2002), pp.542–566.

Žižek, Slavoj and Taek-Gwang Lee, edited, *The Idea of Communism 3: The Seoul Conference* (London & New York: Verso, 2016).

Žižek, Slavoj, Frank Ruda and Agon Hamza, *Reading Marx* (London: Polity Press, 2018).

REFERENCES

Marx's work has a complex editorial history. Throughout this book I have drawn quotations primarily from *The Marx Engels Collected Works* (*MECW*), published by Lawrence and Wishart in 50 volumes. I have also made references to the Penguin editions of Marx's writings. These include: Karl Marx, *Early Writings*, introduced by Lucio Colletti and translated by Rodney Livingstone and Gregor Benton (London: Penguin, 1992); Karl Marx, *The Grundrisse: Foundations of a Critique of Political Economy*, translated and with a foreword by Martin Nicolaus (London: Penguin, 1993); Karl Marx, *Capital: A Critique of Political Economy*, volume 1, introduced by Ernest Mandel and translated by Ben Fowkes (London: Penguin, 1990); Karl Marx *Capital*, volume 2, introduced by Ernest Mandel and translated by David Fernbach (London: Penguin, 1992) and *Capital*, volume 3, introduced by Ernest Mandel and translated by David Fernbach (London: Penguin, 1991). Finally, in my discussion of the *Communist Manifesto* (1848), I have taken quotations from Karl Marx and Friedrich Engels, the *Communist Manifesto*, edited and introduced by David McLellan (Oxford: Oxford World Classics, 1998).

INDEX